the popcorn principles *Strike Back!*

INTERVIEWS WITH SCREENWRITERS WHO ALSO WRITE NOVELS

JOHN GASPARD

ALBERT'S BRIDGE
BOOKS

The Popcorn Principles Strike Back: Interviews With Screenwriters Who Also Write Novels

First Edition | July 2024

https://www.albertsbridgebooks.com

THE AUDIOBOOK

While I believe the interviews which make up this book are a great read, I think the experience is even better if you can hear each of the writers as we discuss screenwriting, TV writing and the impact those skills can have on your novel writing. So here's a link where you can download (for free) the audiobook version of this book: https://BookHip.com/SRFPNGH

Or simply scan the QR code below and start listening!

Otherwise, turn the page and just keep reading. It's great information either way.

CONTENTS

INTRODUCTION

I never dreamed there would be a fourth book in The Popcorn Principles universe.

In fact, I'm sort of amazed there's even one book.

The first one came about because I was often asked—due to my having written and produced low-budget movies <u>and</u> having written a number of novels—what were the crossover points between the two crafts?

That is, what tips had I learned from screenwriting that I went on to use while writing novels?

I knew I had personally learned a lot from my filmmaking experiences that had bled over into novel writing. But I was also fortunate to have interviewed more than a hundred filmmakers (mostly screenwriters and directors) about the process they had gone through to craft their movies. (The interviews were part of four filmmaking books I'd written and an ongoing film blog.)

From these conversations, I recognized the overlaps between how they were telling stories for the screen and which of those ideas would be helpful to novelists.

So, I wrote down the top twenty-five things screenwriters did on a regular basis that might be of help to fiction writers of any stripe.

That became *The Popcorn Principles*.

And then I went back to writing my Eli Marks mystery series, thinking that would be that.

However, people really seemed to like *The Popcorn Principles* and they started asking, "Are there more?"

As it turned out, there was more.

I combed through all the interviews for more pointers. And that became *More Popcorn Principles: The Sequel*, which offered up another score of tips for the aspiring novelist, based on how screenwriters think and write.

At that point I thought my work was done.

But then two things happened.

First: readers wrote and said they liked the writing prompts at the end of each chapter in both books (questions designed to help you take key ideas and integrate them into your work), but they wanted more. Was there a Popcorn Principles workbook? So that became the third book in the series, *The Popcorn Principles Unleashed: A Workbook for Novelists*.

However, at the same time, I was conducting interviews for my podcast, *Behind the Page: The Eli Marks Podcast* (which is a promotional device for my mystery series), and I spoke to two different authors who had connections to my genre: Nicholas Meyer and Dennis Palumbo.

Both were successful screenwriters. Both were also successful novelists.

And so—even though I'd drawn on tons of past interviews for the first three books—here I had two writers who successfully straddled the worlds of filmmaking and novel writing.

They had been there and lived to tell the tale.

Each had their own ideas on how their screenwriting chops had helped them when they made the move from the silver screen into novel writing.

And it turns out, they weren't alone.

In the end, I spoke with a dozen film and TV writers who also wrote novels. And—not so surprisingly—I got a dozen points of view on how their past work in films and TV informed their fiction work.

In the process, they told me about how they got into writing in the first place, the big lessons they learned along the way, and how that experience helped them when they turned to novel writing. (As a bonus, I also got a pretty solid short seminar on how to direct four-camera situation comedies from TV writer and novelist Ken Levine, and a great behind-the-scenes story from Nick Mohammed about *Ted Lasso*.)

The following twelve chapters are those interviews, which you can read in the pages of this book or listen to in the audiobook.

The order of the chapters is simply the order in which I recorded the interviews, from the Fall of 2023 through the Winter/Spring of 2024.

The writers profiled in this book represent a unique intersection of creativity and craft. They have walked the line between the collaborative world of film and television and the solitary pursuit of novel writing. Their insights offer a bridge between these two storytelling mediums, helping novelists benefit from the hard-won lessons of seasoned screenwriters.

So, whether you're an experienced novelist looking for fresh inspiration or an aspiring writer hungry for guidance, I think these interviews provide a treasure trove of wisdom. By learning from those who have mastered the art of storytelling across multiple mediums, I think you'll come out the other end with a sharper skillset and a better understanding of how to tackle your next (or current) project.

So, grab a tub of popcorn, get comfortable, and prepare to be enlightened, entertained and inspired by the experiences of these remarkable storytellers.

NICHOLAS MEYER

Nicholas Meyer is a versatile storyteller who has worked across novels, screenplays, and film directing. He first gained notice in 1971 by writing a non-fiction book which went behind-the-scenes on the making of the film, <u>Love Story</u>.

In 1974, his best-selling mystery novel <u>The Seven-Per-Cent Solution</u>, blended the worlds of Sherlock Holmes and Sigmund Freud in a clever and entertaining way . He went on to write the screenplay adaptation for <u>The Seven-Per-Cent Solution</u> novel, earning an Academy Award nomination. His directing debut came with the time-travel film <u>Time After Time</u> in 1979.

He is well-known for his work revitalizing the Star Trek franchise through films like <u>The Wrath of Khan</u>, <u>The Voyage Home</u>, and <u>The Undiscovered Country</u>. Meyer provided a fresh perspective while still honoring the core essence of Star Trek. This skill at putting a new spin on established properties was also seen in his subsequent Sherlock Holmes novels like <u>The West End Horror</u> and <u>The Canary Trainer</u>.

Meyer believes novelists should be bold in bringing their unique voices and perspectives to their work. His body of work exemplifies that approach, breathing new life into beloved franchises while staying true to what made them appealing in the first place.

As far as I can tell, the first screenplay you wrote would have been your adaptation of *Around the World in 80 Days* as a teenager. Is that about right?

Nicholas Meyer: Yes, if you can call it writing. But, you know, it was almost like notes for a silent movie. Yeah, I started it when I was about eleven or twelve and we finished when I was about seventeen. And we filmed on weekends and school holidays and summer vacations and things like that. And, of course, we shot out of sequence, which means that I grew up and down over that time.

And you're of course playing Fogg.

Nicholas Meyer: I was Fogg. Yes. And the kid who grew up to edit my movies played Passepartout.

Now was this—just to get geeky for a second—was this on the Super 8 format or the regular 8 format?

Nicholas Meyer: It was regular eight and—

Wow.

Nicholas Meyer: --and then there was a magnetic stripe and we added music and narration later.

Okay, so I believe in your memoir somewhere you wrote something like, "Writing was always an unconscious goal." And I know that you wrote several hundred film reviews while in college. I know you went to New York, worked for Paramount in publicity. I know you wrote the "Making of" *Love Story* book, which—

Nicholas Meyer: Another masterpiece.

Well, maybe not, but kind of a smart way to get a foot in the door. And it, if I'm remembering correctly, it gave you enough income to move to LA and starve for a little bit. Is that right?

Nicholas Meyer: Yes, it gave me enough income to starve.

All right. So, now this is where the timeline gets fuzzy for me. Because I'm trying to figure out how many screenplays did you write—produced and unproduced—before you sat down to write *The Seven Percent Solution*?

Nicholas Meyer: Oh, I wrote a lot of screenplays. When I was, I guess, eighteen or something, I was in love with a Jack Finney novel called *Assault on a Queen*. Subsequently made into a very bad movie with Frank Sinatra. But I was still at college at the University of Iowa, and this was my first screenplay, and I just... I didn't have the rights to the book or anything. And I guess in retrospect, you might charitably refer to it as an exercise. But I started on page one and I sort of wrote how that would look as a script and put in dialogue and then on to page two and so on.

The other screenplay of that period that I wrote was a biopic on the life of Heinrich Schliemann. I don't know if you are familiar with Heinrich Schliemann, but he's the guy who discovered Troy. He's in some ways conceded to be the rather messy father of archaeology. He was a self-made guy, very, very rich, became very, very rich. And at the height of his prosperity, decided to pursue a childhood infatuation with *The Iliad*.

And his significant contribution—above and beyond the actual discovery which bore this out—was his thesis that legends and myths have their origins in fact. That there must have been a Troy. There must have been a Camelot. And he taught himself twenty-three languages and he was a bit of a thief and a bit of a liar and stuff. But it was quite a romantic story. The details of which his child bride, blah, blah.

So that was another unproduced. screenplay. At one point, a little later, I tried to interest John Houston in it.

When I got to Hollywood, which was in 1971, I started writing television movies that were getting produced. I wrote *Judge Dee and The Haunted Monastery* for ABC. And my friend Jeremy Kagan, who was the director, took a chance on me as the writer.

And then I wrote, a television movie about the Orson Welles' *War of the Worlds* broadcast, which I wanted to call *The Night the Martians Landed*. But in their wisdom, the network called it *The Night that Panicked America*, which I didn't think was nearly as fun or funny.

Anyway, so I wrote a few TV movies, including some follow up to the first *Judge Dee* movie, but then the actor who played the star died. So that was the end of writing more *Judge Dee* movies. And then the Writer's Guild went on strike right about the time I was sort of hitting my stride there.

Up to that point, had you had any formal training in screen-writing? Or was it just writing 400 movie reviews and seeing a million movies that kind of imbued in you that ability?

Nicholas Meyer: I was in the playwriting workshop at the University of Iowa. The University of Iowa is the home of the Writer's Workshop, which is arguably the most influential center of writing, I guess, in the United States, maybe beyond. Kurt Vonnegut was there while I was there. Gail Godwin was there. You know, previous to that, Philip Roth, Nelson Algren, John Cheever, there's a lot of people.

And my playwriting instructor, Howard Stein, was a great teacher. He was a very mercurial individual, hot tempered, and a lot of things. But I learned. I learned what drama was. And then it was about learning how to translate what I had learned —in terms of theatrical drama, stage drama—to add the pictures. And there I was largely self-taught. I began as a playwright and also somebody who wrote a lot of prose. But I had to teach myself how to reduce the dialogue. And nothing taught me so well as directing a movie.

Right.

Nicholas Meyer: And that movie was *Time After Time*. And what I learned was really how much airspace dialogue could take in what was essentially a kind of a visual medium. And I had to learn to make shorter and shorter speeches. I was very self-taught.

And somebody said—maybe it was Stein, I don't know—watch *Star Trek* and turn off the sound. And you're just seeing talking heads. Watch *Mission Impossible* and turn off the sound. And you're seeing guys lighting fuses or busting safes and stuff like that.

Now reverse it.

Listen to *Star Trek* without watching it. And you're hearing a radio play which works pretty well. But if you listen to *Mission Impossible* on TV, you're hearing... TSSSHHHHH. And, you know, fuses burning and doors slamming and squealing brakes and whatever. So, yeah, I was sort of self-taught in that last lap of learning to become a screenwriter.

Okay, so that takes us to the writer's strike of 1972. I understand that the idea for the Sherlock Holmes novel had been percolating in your mind for a while. I think you had interest in all of his stories as a teenager. What was it that made you decide, "Hey, I'm a screenwriter, I should write a novel"?

Nicholas Meyer: Well, first of all, we weren't allowed to write screenplays. We were only allowed to picket. And the woman with whom I was living at the time said, "Well, now's the perfect time for you to write that Sherlock Holmes meets Sigmund Freud novel that you keep yakking about." And she was right, I had nothing else going on.

And how long had you been yakking about it?

Nicholas Meyer: Years. Years. I started reading the Sherlock Holmes stories when I was about eleven years old. My dad gave me the stories and I wolfed them down. And to say that they made a lasting impression is self-evidently an understatement, since I've now finished my sixth Sherlock Holmes novel.

So, I sat down, and I wrote the novel. And then the novel took a long time to get published. There were a lot of legal things having to do with the Conan Doyle estate. So, I sat down and wrote another novel that didn't have legal problems, which was called *Target Practice*. And that was actually published first, in March of '74. And I believe *The Seven Percent Solution* came out in August of '74. And thereafter was purchased, as a movie. Which I sold on condition that I write the script.

A very smart condition.

Nicholas Meyer: Yes, absolutely. I thought, you know, if anybody's gonna screw it up, I want it to be me.

So, when you sat down to write it—having all these screenplays behind you and having an understanding of drama—how did the screenplays help you, or did they help you at all, in the shaping and execution of that novel?

Nicholas Meyer: Well, a very difficult question for several reasons. One is because you're asking me to recollect events that are probably about, I blush to say, half a century old. I have a good memory. It's a pretty good memory, but it's not a perfect memory. You know, it's not perfect.

But my recollection of writing the novel was I never thought about a movie at all or about screenplays. All I thought about was imitating, to the best of my ability, the style of Arthur Conan Doyle, the creator of Sherlock Holmes. And I had to jump through a lot of hoops to do it. I started trying it on a typewriter, and it just wasn't reading like Holmes. And I realized I was going to have to do this longhand, which is the way Doyle did it. So, I don't think I thought in terms of a screenplay at all.

But when it was time to do the screenplay of the novel, I certainly was thinking: you know, somebody said you have to be ruthless when you're working on any kind of work. You have to be willing to throw away that sunset shot that you spent, you know, hours getting. And then you look at it in the finished movie and it doesn't belong. It slows up the action, whatever. It's a gorgeous shot but forget it. Forget about it.

I found I was able, to a certain degree—maybe not enough, maybe too much—to be ruthless with my own novel, in terms of, translating it into film. I'll give you a couple of examples that I think are pertinent.

One is: there is a tennis match in the novel. And I thought about it in the movie, and I thought, "Gee, this isn't like *Strangers on a Train*, where everything is depending on the outcome of a tennis match. This is an interruption, let's get rid of it."

And Herb Ross—who was the director and who was very good to me throughout this whole process—said, "No, no, no, we can't get rid of the tennis match, everybody loves the tennis match." And I thought, well, that's kind of nuts. But the tennis match is in the movie, and I guess I think it works.

The other thing that I felt when reevaluating the novel, was I saw writing the screenplay as an opportunity to improve the novel. I don't know about you, but if I re-read something of mine six weeks or six months later, I'm dying to get out a pencil and an eraser particularly. And I thought that the first half of my novel worked pretty well. Holmes is addicted to cocaine. Watson needs to get him to Vienna to be treated by this doctor. And then there's a mystery on which they combine forces.

It was the mystery itself that troubled me, and it troubled me for two reasons. One is, I wasn't persuaded that it was a very good mystery. And the other is, that I'd had the experience of going to see the movie of the novel *Presumed Innocent* by Scott Turow. And I had read the book, so I knew who did it. I knew who did it. And I thought... I don't want that experience to happen to the audience of *The Seven Percent Solution*, which was read by at least as many people as read *Presumed Innocent*.

So, I said, okay, I'm going to switch it up and see if I cannot improve this mystery. Which maybe I did.

The other thing, you know, what's the difference between writing a novel and writing a screenplay? And I'm not talking at this point about an adaptation. I'm just saying, what's the difference? The difference, or at least the differences that occur to me, revolve around the fact that when you write a novel, a novel is a totally elastic form, just for starters. It could be long. It could be short. It could be written in the first person. It could be written in the third person. It could even be written in the second person. A novel is a very elastic form.

A screenplay is not.

In a novel, you are in total control. You are the master. You are the creator. You are answerable to nobody, except the yes/no of a publisher. But you get to write it the way you want, and you are only limited by your own abilities.

When you are writing a screenplay, you are writing to order. If you look at the credits, the fine print on a movie, you are not the author. Universal Pictures, for purposes of copyright—Universal, Paramount, Warner Brothers, whoever—is the author of what you wrote. It's work for hire. Someone is paying you the checks.

Obviously, there's one big exception: You write a spec script, then you are in total control ... until the point that you sell it. And people may want changes that you may or may not agree to make. Some directors have final cut over their movies. I don't know that a lot of screenwriters do. I think Paddy Chayefsky had it so no one could change a word at a certain point. And I'm not sure that was a good thing either.

But it's a difference in control. And writing work for hire and writing work to satisfy yourself.

So, when you wrote the screenplay for *The Seven Percent Solution*, at that point had you already written the second Holmes book, *The West End Horror*?

Nicholas Meyer: Can't remember.

Okay. Let's broaden the question a little bit. Having written the screenplay for that one, did that process, do you think it had any impact on how you wrote the subsequent novels?

Nicholas Meyer: No, the novels are always about imitating Doyle. The fact that I have a sort of cinematic sensibility may—on a kind of unconscious level—inform some of the visual elements of the books. But I was not ever thinking of them as screenplays while I was writing them. I don't think—I could be deceiving myself—but I don't think so.

I also think, and going back to your earlier question, I think I wrote the screenplay for *The Seven Percent Solution* — No, I think I wrote *The West End Horror* before I wrote the screenplay. *The West End Horror* was already another bestseller when I was working on the screenplay, because Universal also optioned that novel at the same time.

But we never got that movie.

Nicholas Meyer: We did not.

Alright, so, as you move forward and you're going back and forth between writing and directing movies. And also working on the Holmes novels, recognizing that you're trying to imitate the best of Doyle. But at the same time, you're also out there making movies and creating visuals and writing screenplays.

So, I'm wondering, do you think, consciously or unconsciously, because in a movie exposition has to be delivered in a cleverer way than it might be in a novel, has that influenced the way you're delivering exposition in a novel? Or is it affecting the way you bring in dialogue, how much you have? I know you've talked about liking speeches. Has it had any impact at all on the novel side?

Nicholas Meyer: I don't think so is the short answer. As I said earlier, when I have the Doyle hat on—and I've written at least one novel, *Confessions of a Homing Pigeon*, which is a sort of autobiographical fiction—I don't think I was thinking of movies then. I think I just, you know, wondered if anybody would want to read this. But it was a novel that I felt at the time that I sort of had to write.

I think on an unconscious level, I may think of sequences that you would call cinematic. You know, in *The Return of the Pharaoh*, they're in a huge sandstorm, there are a lot of cinematic illusions and possibilities. But I'm only sort of half, I'm not thinking of the movie. I'm only thinking of how it looks on the page.

But do you think—I'm not suggesting that you're writing a movie when you write the novel—but I just think you can't help but become a better visual storyteller on the page if you've tried to sell a visual idea to somebody in a movie. So, when you go to write the novels, it's like "Here's probably a better way to describe this that the reader is going to get right away." "Or here's a better way to get into the scene."

One of the things you learn right away in screenwriting, and it's the oldest trope there is, but it's that you should get into the scene as late as you possibly can and get out as soon as you possibly can. And screenwriters know that. And I think the better novelists know that.

But if they don't know that, they can learn that from watching a movie and going, "Oh, I don't need that much setup. I really can just jump right into the scene, and it's actually going to be better if I jump right in." And I think that's something screenwriters have to do that novelists could learn from.

Nicholas Meyer: Well, I think novel writing has changed as a result of movies. First of all, we now have graphic novels, which are like storyboarded novels. And I certainly have learned that the people who read novels now are not enamored of super lengthy descriptions. Because we've now seen so much visually you know, if I say it looked like X, or some analogy, people can sort of piece it together and do a lot of that work for you.

Whereas something that Melville or Dickens might write—Melville wrote travelogs, because people couldn't go to the Marquesas, and they couldn't go to places. Nowadays, you just get on your computer, go online, and you'll get videos of whatever you want to see. And that has certainly changed writing description for sure.

Well, it's that idea that you said. It's the idea of *just enough,* **which is something we learn as screenwriters because we have to keep people reading the script. I think William Goldman, in** *Adventures in the Screen Trade,* **said that he described a room as smelling of gun oil. And he said, "I could have written two paragraphs on that, but that's all the production designer needed was the room smells of gun oil." And he or she was able to go off and create that.**

And learning to write just enough to give the people who are reading the screenplay the information they need to do their job also, I think, translates into novel writing, where there is a tendency to, sometimes, as you said, people over describe. And learning to write *just enough* **is kind of a skill.**

Nicholas Meyer: The other way to look at this, and I once had the opportunity of, asking Billy Wilder about this. I said, "In a lot of your movies, there's a narrator. There's a voiceover. And why do you find yourself doing that?"

And he said, "Two reasons." He said, "A narrator allows me to jump through a lot of exposition really fast, and get into the story much faster, much quicker." And secondly, he said, "I'm a satirist. And the narrator allows me to comment on the action."

So that's another way of cutting through description and exposition, is to have somebody say, you know, "I hadn't sold a screenplay..." you know, whatever Joe Gillis says in *Sunset Boule-*

vard. "I spoke to a couple of yes men at Metro. To me, they said no."

That's Wilder. So, you mentioned the sandstorm in *Pharaoh*, and it's a fantastic sequence. And I remember when we talked about it, I had thought it was based on an actual event. And you explained, no, that those sorts of things did happen, but that you'd made that one up.

And that got us talking about the mixing of fact and fiction in semi-fiction: you know, the things that you wrote in *The Seven Percent Solution* that were true about Freud. Even though Holmes wasn't a real character, Freud was a real person. So, what you're writing is historical fiction, and I know you do a lot of research. I imagine you have, for the latest book, several stacks of yellow legal pads with notes on getting things right.

As a novelist, when you're writing quote unquote "fiction," how much of an obligation do you feel toward getting things right like that?

Nicholas Meyer: That's a very hard to answer question. Somebody said, "I don't know how to define pornography, but I know it when I see it."

I feel—and I'm not sure obligation is the right word—but I feel something like an obligation—when I'm writing a Holmes story and fitting him into history—to kind of make it plausible or possible and get as much of the surrounding stuff right. But if it involves rerouting a train line a little bit or fudging a couple of dates a little bit, I go, okay, it's make believe. But I want it to be accurate enough so that the flavor of the events being depicted is plausible in a general kind of way.

I'm not writing a newspaper, which somebody described as the first draft of history. I'm trying to interweave, without doing a mammoth injustice.

I'll give you an example of a troubling injustice. A lot of people who no longer read—and who no longer read history and don't know anything about it—went and saw a movie called *The Deer Hunter*, which was a very celebrated movie. And in that movie, we are told that the North Vietnamese forced American POWs to play Russian roulette. Well, they didn't. There's not a single documented case.

And to me, that represents stepping over the line. It may be good drama. But in an era when people are getting their history from the movies, I don't think you can go that far. Because now we're, quote, learning history, in quotation marks, from this movie. And the movie gets a lot of things right. So, we think, "Oh yes, this is what happened, they really did this."

But it's not helpful. It may reinforce prejudices and xenophobia and all kind of hatred of the unknown and the enemy and the other. But it didn't happen. And I think that was irresponsible of the filmmakers.

So even in fiction there's a moral responsibility.

Nicholas Meyer: I feel one. I don't say there is. I can only speak for myself.

But on the other hand, and this is an example you gave me the last time we talked, Queen Elizabeth and Mary, Queen of Scots never met. Yet, as you said, in the 6,000 plays, movies, operas, books about it...

Nicholas Meyer: ...they always meet. They always meet. But I don't think that depicting that meeting serves—like the Russian roulette example—to reinforce unfortunate prejudices.

And you can say at the end, by the way, they never met. When you look at the opening of the Lawrence Olivier *Richard III* movie, there is a preamble in somewhat flowery language, the viewer is informed: "Okay. A lot of this is legend and not necessarily a fact." In other words, the Richard III that you are about to meet in this movie who is depicted is the worst scumbag ever, may not have been all those things. Or any of them.

There's actually a Stephen Freer's movie called *The Lost King*, which is about the woman who discovered the skeletal remains of Richard III in a parking lot. And you learn—I learned this a long time ago—that there is a Ricardian society of people who want to restore the good name of Richard III.

Remember, that the person writing the play, Shakespeare, was writing for the granddaughter of the man who killed Richard III, who was now the Queen of England. So, Henry VII was the usurper. But it probably wouldn't have served Shakespeare very well to depict Elizabeth's grandfather as a usurper. Didn't make her look good. So, he wrote like the worst guy he could come up with. And, of course, that's the worst guy ever. But it's not necessarily true.

And at least the Olivier movie pays a kind of lip service to telling the audience, you know, this makes a good story. But it's not necessarily a true story. The Italians have this phrase, *Se non è vero è ben trovato.* "It may not be true, but it's well told."

For aspiring novelists, do you have any piece of advice that you'd give them, based on your experience both in screenwriting and in novel writing? If you're starting out to write something, what's a good thing to know?

Nicholas Meyer: Well, I think the good thing to know is Be Very Bold.

If you're just going to write a novel that's like somebody else writes it, why bother? Let them do it. You know, the Doyle thing is obviously a big exception. But Doyle isn't around, so I'm helping him out.

All you have to offer as an artist, any kind of artist, is yourself. And if yourself is not interesting enough and if you don't believe in all of that, then don't do it. Don't just write pale imitations. Or even if you are writing an imitation, find a way to make it your own.

That's what I did with the *Star Trek* movies. And that's what I do with the Holmes books, because you think you have something to offer and being bold and not second guessing yourself.

But if you're writing a novel, write the novel that you would want to read.

DENNIS PALUMBO

Dennis Palumbo is a multi-talented writer who first made a name for himself as a Hollywood screenwriter, penning scripts for hit TV shows like <u>Welcome Back, Kotter</u> and the beloved comedy film <u>My Favorite Year</u>. He was also publishing mystery short stories in places like <u>Ellery Queen's Mystery Magazine</u> right from the start of his screenwriting career.

After retiring from TV and movies, Palumbo switched gears and became a licensed psychotherapist. However, he kept writing—exploring the psychological side of the creative life in his acclaimed non-fiction book, <u>Writing From the Inside Out</u>, as well as penning the Daniel Rinaldi thriller series of novels.

In the interview, he highlights how his screenwriting background informs his crisp dialogue and ability to maintain narrative momentum. But he also discusses utilizing subtext and trusting the reader—skills honed from his screenwriting career that elevate his prose.

What first got you into TV writing and screenwriting?

Dennis Palumbo: Well, I guess it's when I graduated from Pitt with an English degree, everybody said, "Well, you can teach or you can do advertising." So, I did advertising. I started to write TV and radio commercials, but I'd always loved film and television. And so, I came out to Los Angeles and partnered with a very, very talented comedy writer named Mark Evanier. And together we got into the sitcom writing business.

We had written a spec episode of *MASH*, and luckily Gene Reynolds, as always happens, they liked the writing, but of course we couldn't write their show because no one has their voice. But he did make some recommendations for agents and as it turned out, I had spent the year before traveling the country with Gabe Kaplan, writing his stand-up act with him.

Oh, wow.

Dennis Palumbo: Yeah, he had seen me at The Comedy Store because I was trying to break in as a writer and no one would hire me. So, I thought, well, so many producers and executives go to The Comedy Store, I'll just get up and do material. And so I had pretty good material. But I didn't have the killer instinct that you need to have as a comic, you know. But Kaplan saw my work and he said, "Come on the road with me."

So, I did. And so, after about eight months on the road with him, there was a story editor working on *Welcome Back, Kotter* named Garry Shandling. And he was in a terrible car accident that laid him up for like eight months (which was a real Road to Damascus experience for him, because after he got out of the hospital, he decided he wanted to be a stand-up comic).

But that meant there was a hole there. They were looking for a story editor on *Welcome Back, Kotter*. So, my writing partner, Mark and I, went in and got that job. Our first writing job was actually the first episode of *Love Boat*. We did one of the segments on that. But our first staff job was on *Welcome Back, Kotter.*

And so, Mark and I were sitcom writers for a couple years. And then he wanted to go into animation, which he did, and was very successful at it. And I wanted to go into features. And so, after doing a couple more sitcoms, I was lucky enough to go in and pitch and sell what became *My Favorite Year.*

So, at that point, did you have any real formal training in TV writing?

Dennis Palumbo: I was an English major and all my training was in prose. When I was in college, I thought I was going to be a novelist. And in fact, it's interesting because I always liked writing prose. And the week that Mark and I got hired on *Welcome Back, Kotter*, was the exact same week I sold my first mystery short story to *Ellery Queen's Mystery Magazine.*

So, throughout my 17 years as a film and TV writer, I kept writing mystery short stories that were getting published. Because I always knew I wanted to write mysteries. And so, it's an interesting thing that—after about fourteen, thirteen years in showbiz—I was in therapy and I started falling in love with the process.

So, I went back to school at night. I didn't tell anyone. I was sort of like Bruce Wayne by day, Batman by night. And nobody knew, but I was taking classes and I was an intern at a psych hospital and a low-fee family clinic. And ultimately, after about seventeen years in the business and I was very, very fortunate, I mean, not only with *My Favorite Year*, but, *K9* and, *White Water Summer* and a bunch of other things I worked on. I was very fortunate.

But I realized I wanted to change my life. So, once I had enough credits and had a graduate degree in counseling, I retired from film and television and began work as a therapist in private practice. But, because I had been a television and film writer, I specialized in working with creative people, primarily writers.

And that's how I built my practice.

Okay. Let's back up a little bit There's a couple things we need to touch on here that are I think really great. The last time we spoke, you talked about your own Road to Damascus moment, which I think was on Ventura Boulevard. Was that right?

Dennis Palumbo: It was on La Cienega. I was with a producer at a restaurant. I don't even know if it's there anymore. It was on Sunset Boulevard, called Le Dome. And I remember talking to this producer, because he wanted me to write this movie for him. And I kept looking at my watch, because I knew I had to go down to a private psychiatric hospital called A Touch of Care, where I was leading a group of schizophrenics in doing role play (which was a lot of fun doing improv and role play with floridly psychotic people. It was very wonderful).

But I kept looking at my watch and finally—after lunch—I'm zooming down La Cienega and I think, you know, I couldn't wait to get out of that lunch, and I can't wait to go where I'm going. I think I want to change my life.

At that moment, I decided, okay. But I really wasn't sure. I had all the credits and I had all the intern hours. All I had to do was just leave show business and start being a therapist. But I wasn't quite ready to pull the trigger. But when I did that, I realized, okay, I do want to change my life.

And so, I had this bizarre ten minutes on the phone where I called my agent, my manager, my business manager, and my lawyer, and I fired all of them. And I said, "It's nothing to do with you guys. I'm now a therapist." And you could hear their jaws dropping on the phone. And so I went into private practice. But I never stopped writing. I was always writing articles and short stories.

So, let's back up. You're writing for TV, and you decide you also want to write a novel, *City Wars*. What was your process? You're a professional writer at that point. Did that make it any easier to get that novel sold?

Dennis Palumbo: Well, here's the funny thing. I had written a bunch of short stories in college, obviously. But when I was on *Kotter*, after about a year, I remember telling my agent, I don't even know if I can write a sentence because we're all sitting around a room pitching Horshack jokes. And you start to wonder, is this writing or funny talking?

And so just as an experiment, I wrote a short story that takes place in the future. And I gave it to my agent, the late Stu Robinson. To his credit, he said, "I think this should be expanded to a novel." And so, he called an editor he knew at Bantam Books. She read the short story, and they hired me to write it as a novel.

So, I had this weird just jump right into the novel writing world overnight, essentially.

Yes, but with your background, as an English major writing prose, that helped a little bit. The short stories that you were writing then, I assume, are the ones that were collected in *From Crime to Crime*?

Dennis Palumbo: Yeah, some of them are collected in *From Crime to Crime*, which is a collection of new and old short stories. Again, I've had such a checkered career. The first short story I ever wrote was a science fiction story that Forrest Ackerman bought for ten dollars. There was this European sci fi character named Perry Rhodan, and Forry Ackerman published the American versions in paperback. But to make sure the books were thick enough he'd throw a couple short stories on the back. And it was the first short story I ever actually sold, before the one I sold to *Ellery Queen*.

Paradoxically, 25 years later when he [Forrest Ackerman] did an anthology of his favorite sci fi short stories, my short story was in there. And I looked at the names and the table of contents, and I was the only person I'd never heard of. But he always liked that story.

You finished the novel, you're working on *Welcome Back, Kotter*, you're doing other series, and then you go in and you pitch *My Favorite Year*. For the one millionth time, would you tell me what that process was?

Dennis Palumbo: Yeah, I'll give you the one-minute version, because the 25-minute version I'm weeping by the end of it. The one-minute version is I went in, and I pitched it to a producer named Mike Gruskoff And it was based on my father's love of Errol Flynn.

When I was a kid, there was *The Late, Late Show*. You're too young to remember this, but there was *The Late, Late Show* on regular television. It came on like at one in the morning, after which there would be the flag and Pledge of Allegiance. And then right after, *The Late, Late Show* would come on. My dad would wake me up, because it would be on a school night, and he would take me down to the TV. We had the volume on super low, so my mother wouldn't hear it. We had to put our faces up against the TV screen, and I watched the *Adventures of Robin Hood* and four or five swashbuckling kinds of movies.

My dad was the number one Errol Flynn fan. And so, I always wondered what it would be like if I could bring Errol Flynn home to meet my dad.

And so, when I went into my Gruskoff meeting, we ended up talking, talking, talking. And I finally said, "Well, I was a young writer on *Welcome Back, Kotter*. How about if we do a show that's like *Your Show of Shows* and Errol Flynn's the guest and I have to squire him around?" Anyway, that's how it happened.

I wrote the first draft, and then the producer showed it to Mel Brooks. He and I did not have a good working relationship, and he was very big at the time. It was *Blazing Saddles* and *Young Frankenstein*, stuff I loved, by the way. Without going into a lot of detail, it was very difficult between the two of us.

I ended up leaving the project and it went into turnaround. I had written it for Peter O'Toole, but by then Peter O'Toole was not someone who moved the needle. And so, Fox offered it to Michael Caine, who passed. Then they offered it to Albert Finney, who not only passed but said, "Who you want is Peter O'Toole."

So it went into turnaround, which means it was now available for some other studio to buy. And then four years later, Peter O'Toole got nominated as Best Actor for *The Stuntman*, and he was bankable for like three months. So, MGM had *My Favorite Year*. By then another writer had come on—Norman Steinberg, a really good writer—had come on to work on the script and Peter O'Toole was attached.

Funnily enough, two movies came out from MGM that summer that everybody thinks were hits. One was *Victor/Victoria*, with Julie Andrews and Robert Preston. The other was *My Favorite Year*. Both were bombs. Nobody went to see either of those movies. But about ten years later, cable TV came out, and most people who've seen *My Favorite Year* have seen it on television.

There was something called the Z Channel, which was one of the first cable channels. And it would take two or three movies and show them continuously for a whole week. Like, I remember *seeing 2001: A Space Odyssey* twenty-five times in a row. Well, they ran *My Favorite Year* twenty-five times during the week. And so now the film is very, very well known. The AFI lists it as one of the 100 best comedies of all time. It's on a lot of people's Ten Best lists. Nobody saw it in the theater.

All right. So, we're getting to the merging point here, where you have left, essentially, show business. You are a full-time psychotherapist, but you are still connected to show business in that you're writing your monthly column for the Writer's Guild magazine—which I have to tell you, that was the thing that when I was getting the magazine (back when I was an active Guild writer), that was the first thing I turned to, because it was always great. You'd read it and go, "Okay, I'm not alone. I'm not alone. Everyone else has this thing." I imagine it was a pretty popular column.

Dennis Palumbo: Well, here's the funny thing about it. The editor used to do a poll every year. And my column, *The Writer's Life,* was always the most popular part of the magazine. Which thrilled me, because I was a working therapist then. And I was talking about the issues writers struggle with: procrastination, loneliness, alienation, writer's block, all that stuff.

I go to a WGA Christmas party and one of the board members comes up to me, this is like four or five years into the column. He said, "Hey, I'm one of your defenders on the board." And I said, "I didn't know I had any attackers." He said, "Oh yeah, every year we vote whether or not to kick your column out of the magazine."

And I said, "Really?" He said, "Yeah, a lot of the board members think it's a mistake to show Hollywood that writers have emotional struggles." And I said, "I don't think that's going to be a surprise to anyone."

But it turned out, there was a little bit of a power struggle involved in keeping my column in the magazine. The column never said, you know, "Here's how you write a scene." It was about here's how you psychologically survive being a writer.

And they felt that the DGA (Director's Guild of America) magazine didn't have anything about the struggles that directors had. And so, it was quite funny to me. But I'll never forget, "I'm one of your defenders on the board." My God, who knew I had attackers?

Okay. So, you're a full-time psychotherapist. I imagine you're still writing short stories at that time. Is that right?

Dennis Palumbo: Oh yeah, I'm always writing short stories. I've had about 25 of them published in different magazines: *The Strand, Ellery Queen,* and many anthologies. And then I have that collection, *From Crime to Crime.*

Also, my columns are collected in a book called *Writing From the Inside Out.* That book shocked me, it's success around the world has been a shock to me.

Why was it a shock to you? The columns had been so popular.

Dennis Palumbo: Who cares about what this one therapist thinks about how writers and creative people should deal with their psychological issues?

Apparently, there's a composition professor at Oxford that emailed me and said, "Oh, I use your book." It's now being used in about 200 universities and colleges and writing programs around the world. It's been out for twenty-five years. It's always in print.

And the response from people who aren't writers, who say to me, "I still found it of value. Because I procrastinate." Or I have a lot of anxiety, or "I have a lot of anxiety when I'm going to pitch something.'

I just assumed a bunch of, you know, knobby headed little TV and film writers like me would read the book. But it turned out to be kind of a surprise to me. And it is still being taught all over the place now.

I think any creative person is going to get a benefit out of reading that book.

Dennis Palumbo: Well, that's very kind of you to say. Like I said, I'm not being fake modest. I'm absolutely surprised that it's still in print and that it's still being taught.

Okay, so now this is where the rubber meets the road. So, you're writing the short stories, you're starting to write novels. Can you think about any points when your screenwriting skills have helped you in structuring or in creating a character or exposition?

Dennis Palumbo: Well, I think it's been invaluable for a number of ways. Number one, one of the things I take pride in with my books is the dialogue. And that all came from my screenwriting life.

And also, my books have a lot of pace. The chapters are like two or three pages long and the books move like rockets. Because I learned about momentum and clarity and pace by writing television and film, where you had to get a lot of information in very quickly.

And the other thing is, I like using short, but very, very pithy descriptions, which I also learned from writing screenplays. You know, in a screenplay, you don't go: "Interior room. Well, there's three windows. There's two chairs. There's, you know, four bureaus. There's a lot of dust ..."

You don't write that. You write something like, "You wouldn't want to stay here one night longer than you had to." Period.

Since my Daniel Rinaldi novels are in first person, he gets to describe things like that. So, I might say something like, you know, "The maître d came over, he looked like an oil slick on stilts," or whatever. I have this real vivid descriptive aspect in the books. And I think that all comes from the economy that you learn writing screenplays.

Well, you know, when you're writing a screenplay you don't have a lot of page space to put that sort of stuff in. But you also have to put in the key information that the department heads are going to have to have, in order to execute it properly.

And by saying, "It's a room you wouldn't want to spend any time in," that's probably far more effective than you writing a long description of it, because you're not going to be the one who is designing that room, but you've told them exactly what they need to come up with.

Dennis Palumbo: Also remember, the first readers of those scripts are not production designers. They're executives. And you have to almost tell them how they're supposed to feel.

If you look at guys like Ron Bass and William Goldman, they were very good in their scripts in telling you how you're supposed to feel. The reason they need to do that is—and I've worked with a lot of really good executives and producers—but many of them don't understand subtext.

I remember I wrote a script where a kid's dad sends him across the sea, because he got expelled from school. And I have a scene where he's sitting on the deck of the ship. It's a period thing. And he's weeping. And the executive at Tristar said, "Why is he crying?" And so, I had to put in, "He's weeping because he's been sent from everything he's ever known from the family he grew up in into a foreign country where he doesn't even speak the language." And the executive says, "Now I get it."

Now to me, if I'm the director, I read that and I rub it all out. I don't need to be told what he thinks. You have to assume—and William Goldman used to say this—that the executives don't get subtext. So, it's not a bad idea to sort of tell them, "This is how you should feel."

And remember, too, as a producer once said to me, "You're not writing a movie. You're writing a screenplay a studio will buy."

So, you could write, "This is the kind of hotel room you wouldn't want to spend one night in." But if you're talking to the production designer, you can talk all you want to about how it should look. Now, by the end of his career, Goldman had gotten so lean and mean, he would go: Interior. Hotel Room. Shitty. Period.

That's all he would write. But you have to also understand by the time you're William Goldman, you don't have to sell much, particularly because he's so good with dialogue. And screenplays are structure plus dialogue.

Do you think novels are the same?

Dennis Palumbo: I think today's novels are the same. Today's novels have the pace of movies and television, if they're thrillers.

It's the rare successful novel that doesn't have a pretty, pretty octane-driven pace. When you read novels from the 30s and 40s, as great as they are, they're a little slow by our standards.

The writing is so gorgeous. Like if you read *The Maltese Falcon*, after the first chapter where he finds out Miles Archer's been murdered, the second chapter is Sam Spade rolling a cigarette, sitting at the side of his bed. An editor would take that out now. But it tells us everything we need to know about him. He's not going to run off halfcocked. He's going to be thinking while he's rolling this cigarette. It's a beautiful moment, but it stops everything. Well, you couldn't do that today. There's no editor that would let that happen today.

That's too bad.

Dennis Palumbo: I agree.

But that's where we are. So, one of the things that I feel like I really got a good handle on by writing screenplays—and by producing what I was writing—was being clever with exposition. You had to do that in TV all the time, because you only had 22 minutes. And you had established things. How do you think you carried that over into novel writing, particularly when you're doing a first-person novel?

Dennis Palumbo: Well, again, the good news about a first-person novel is your exposition is all happening in your narrator's head. And so, because the books all take place in my hometown of Pittsburgh, one of the joys for me is describing how the city has changed.

My hero has been part of the old Pittsburgh, where the steel mills were, where I worked. He's now in the new Pittsburgh. He wears a jacket and tie. He's a psychologist. He's the first member of his family to go to college. So, he can talk about what he's looking at with a point of view.

You can do a lot of exposition as long as you have a point of view. So, he can talk about the new steel and glass towers that are in Pittsburgh, but they loom over cobblestone streets that still have streetcar tires and all the mills are gone. So, any new steel that is used to build anything in Pittsburgh is imported from Japan. So, it's exposition, but it's also through his point of view about how everything is changing.

And so, I think one of the ways you get away with exposition is, number one, if you can do it, put it in dialogue. Because people like reading dialogue. They don't like reading long expositions. But if you're going to do exposition, do it like Cormac McCarthy. Let it have a point of view.

Or bury it in a joke. You could say, "The last time I saw you, you were talking to a divorce lawyer." And he could say, "No, that was two marriages ago. And three different divorce lawyers." Boom, boom, boom. We now know who this guy is, and we haven't said a word.

Oh, and it's such a cleaner way of doing that.

Dennis Palumbo: Yeah, and I love dialogue. So, my books tend to be somewhat dialogue heavy, because I like writing it.

One of the favorite lines—when I was talking to Nick Meyer —that he said was from *Sunset Boulevard*. "I talked to the Yes Men at Metro. To me, they said no." And that told you all you really needed to know about what was going on in William Holden's life.

Dennis Palumbo: Well, what I like is William Goldman's screenplay for *Harper*, where he's talking to Lauren Bacall, because he's looking for her kidnapped husband. And he said, "Well, I hope we find him." And she said, "No, I don't care if you find him alive or dead. Actually, I want him dead. I'd like to dance on his grave." And then she goes, "Do I shock you, Mr.

Harper?" He goes, "Well people in love say funny things." I've always loved that line.

When it comes to creating characters and getting characterization, when you were working in TV and movies, you had an advantage that you just had to do the first half and the actors would bring a lot to it. But I'm sure you learned some stuff doing that, that has helped you with the Rinaldi books and the people he meets. Do you see any instances where that's sort of history has helped on your half?

Dennis Palumbo: Yeah, because when I was a TV and film writer, it always helped me to envision the actor who would be playing the role. For example, in my Daniel Rinaldi novels, as soon as I was working on the police sergeant, Harry Polk, I thought, this is Jerry Orbach from *Law and Order*. And, once I knew that that's who he was, I had the cadence of the way he talked.

I have a similar character in the Eli Marks series. There is a cop who is, the voice is totally taken from James Gregory from *Barney Miller*.

Dennis Palumbo: Oh. What a great actor.

Great character actor, just great.

Dennis Palumbo: Yeah. And so, with Daniel Rinaldi, he's a composite of a couple people. Because he's a former amateur boxer, I didn't want him to be that soft male that we know, Alan Alda as a therapist. I think of him as Liam Neeson as a therapist. And, you know, so he's a touchy-feely guy that looks like a boxer. And that helped me visualize him as being a little more edgy, a little more, ballsy than we traditionally think of male therapists.

And, in terms of his humor and his maverick approach to clinical work, he's just a brave version of me. Because I'm very snarky about diagnoses and the way the mental health system in America works and the insurance companies and the DSM and all these things that I think are not great. And so, the Daniel Rinaldi character allows me to be snarky about all that stuff.

In thinking back on it, are there any other tricks from your screenwriting and TV writing days that you think you're using when you sit down to start a new novel?

Dennis Palumbo: Yes. The most important thing I think that I got from writing screenplays is start the scene way in. Don't have someone come in and go, "Hello, how are you? You want a cup of coffee?" No, start the scene with, "What do you mean, where did I get the gun?" And end it without any resolution.

In other words, there's a tendency for new writers to go, well, then they have somebody fight and debate, and at the end, well, "Okay, I guess you're right." You never want to do that. You always want to end the scene with, "Well, do your best to convince me, but I bet you won't." Cut To: now they're in the truck driving down the road going, "How the fuck did he convince me?"

Less is more. But more importantly, what I learned that I use in my novels is, get into the scene deeper at the beginning and get out of it faster on a button: on a question or a hook.

My favorite example of that is from *Michael Clayton*, a film I really love. He's talking to a guy who's going to be in trouble and he's like a fixer. And the phone rings and he says, "Do you think that's the police?" And Clayton goes, "They never call first."

And that's the end of the scene, but we know the cops are coming. I love "They never call first." That should be the last line of your chapter if you're writing that as a novel.

One of the things that you do so nicely—and it's tied to that —is as you're reading, you want to get to the end of the chapter. And you want to go to sleep. But no, because you've left us with a cliffhanger.

Dennis Palumbo: I always try to end the chapter with a hook And that's what I learned from not only film, but in sitcoms: you go out with a joke. And it's always nice if it's a reversal: "Well, the last thing I'm going to do is follow you into that tunnel." Next chapter: "God, it's colder in here in this tunnel than I thought it would be."

That jump takes away the need to tell the audience how he talked them into it, because the reader, by that point, wants them to go in the tunnel.

Is there a principle from filmmaking and screenwriting that you think is undervalued or overlooked in novel writing?

Dennis Palumbo: I think probably trusting the reader.

In movies, a good screenplay really trusts the audience to get subtext. Like I said in that story I told you about TriStar, a director would cut out all that stuff. And an actor would cut out all that stuff. A good actor, if it says, a line, and then it says, "Upset," the good actor will cross out any descriptor, because he doesn't want to be told how he's going to feel when that camera's rolling.

I think there's a certain brevity that allows you to trust the reader. Now, you don't want to be so lean and mean that you don't feel grounded, that you don't feel like you're there. But, you know, we're all the children of Elmore Leonard and James

Ellroy: There ain't a whole lot around it, you know what I mean? And you're just hurdled along. But those guys are tacticians when it comes to dialogue.

I think *The Friends of Eddie Coyle* is the greatest crime novel. It's all dialogue. The first sentence of that book, "Jackie Brown, at 25, said he could get them some guns." That's the first sentence. We don't know Jackie Brown. Who's he talking to? Who's he talking about? It doesn't matter. And we're off. And it's all dialogue. But you've got to write like George V. Higgins if you're going to do that.

You had the advantage that—sometimes—all you had was dialogue, because it's two characters in a room and it's the same set we've seen every week. What are you going to do differently? You also had the advantage, at least with *Welcome Back, Kotter*, you'd written for Gabe's voice, and you knew that going in.

Dennis Palumbo: I knew his voice going in, though—paradoxically—the person I most identified with was Horshack. So, I tended to write most of the Horshack jokes.

But it also helps to be honest. When you're on a sitcom, you're in a room with five, six, seven other really funny people. And I felt I was the least funny person in the room. What I tended to try to remind people is, well, what would he actually feel? And then the funny people would say a funny version of what he would feel.

But using the feeling as the basis for the joke.

Dennis Palumbo: Yes, as the basis. Yeah, because there is a tendency, if you're not careful in sitcoms, to just have a character say a joke because it's a joke. And it may get a big laugh, but it doesn't help you much.

Right. And you'll probably end up cutting it.

Dennis Palumbo: Yes, you'll wind up cutting it, because it takes you away from the emotional arc of the scene.

Let's end with just a quick commercial for the book, *Writing From the Inside Out*. The audience listening to this or reading this, are novelists or aspiring novelists. What do you think they'd get out of looking through that book?

Dennis Palumbo: I think they would feel less alone. The primary thing—and I get emails and calls from people all over the world from this book—is that everybody's anxious. Everybody worries if they're any good. If you write something really great, you worry about what if it's not so great the next day? Will anyone like this? Can I make a living from it? Should I work with a partner? What do I think about money?

To me, the purpose of the book is to make you feel you are enough right now to be the writer you want to be. With all of your doubts and fears and insecurities.

I remember one time a patient said, "I'd like to take all of my doubts and insecurities and neuroses and throw them outside and just sit down and write." And I said, "Write about what?" You got to invite all of those back in, because that's the human condition.

The other thing that is really important for starting writers to understand is that every successful writer they admire used to be a struggling writer. And in my practice, I have enormously successful writers—and they still struggle. They still have act two problems. They still worry that the ending doesn't work. They still worry that they're repeating themselves. They worry that their agent's getting bored. They're worried that they can't keep up with the trends.

No matter what your level of success, if you're a real artist, you're always worried. Only hacks don't worry.

Yes. Who was it who said that the only people who don't have the imposter syndrome are imposters?

Dennis Palumbo: Yes, that's exactly right. Thomas Mann said it the best: "Writers are people for whom writing is more difficult than it is for other people." And that's exactly the truth. The more of a professional you are, the more glum you're going to be.

LAWRENCE ALLAN

Lawrence Allan is a multi-talented writer who has made his mark across novels, plays, screenplays and even Pakistani television serials. Though born and raised in the American Midwest, Allan's creative talents have taken him around the world and into numerous storytelling mediums.

He first gained acclaim as a playwright, with works like <u>Umbrella</u>, <u>Fallout</u>, and <u>The Lunar Adventures of Dar and Matey</u> receiving Off-Broadway and regional productions. His noir comedy novel <u>Big Fat F@!k Up</u> was a finalist for the Shamus Award for Best First PI Novel and winner of two Claymore Awards, announcing Allan as a fresh literary voice.

No matter the format, Allan brings a distinctly humorous, character-driven sensibility to his work, with protagonists that use laughter to deflect from deep emotional trauma. His skills were sharpened through top-tier training at institutions like The University of Texas at Austin, The University of Iowa, and improv/theatrical schools in Minneapolis and California.

Allan's extensive background in improv, playwriting and screen-writing greatly influenced his transition into novel writing. His experience honing crisp dialogue, keeping narratives energetic, and allowing stories to discover themselves proved invaluable when tackling his debut novel's mystery plot.

What first drew you to writing and how did you get started in the industry?

Lawrence Allan: My earliest memory of writing would be when I did my own comic book adaptation of *The Empire Strikes Back*. I think I might have literally copied pages from the comic book adaptation I had of *The Empire Strikes Back*. So, my first act of writing was to steal.

Which they say is a very good idea: you should copy until you learn how to do it yourself.

Lawrence Allan: Yeah. I think when I started taking it more seriously—as seriously as anyone could take being in high school—was high school writing. I had an AP composition class, and I was already a theater kid. So, I was already performing.

And so, in the AP composition class, there were other good friends of mine. And I remember—I don't know if I was writing short stories at that point or not, I might have been—but I was also a big reader. But I remember one of the assignments—you would do it in groups—was to create like a literary magazine. And I think my group, we got really competitive. So, we had so much content. So many different short stories. It was like a journal. And I had like three or four things in it; I was the editor, so I could accept my own work. So probably then.

And then, I went to college, University of Iowa, for theater. Of course, it's well known for its prose writing department, but it's theater department was fairly well regarded as well.

My freshman year is when I started playwriting. I took a play-writing class, and I had a teacher who encouraged me, "Oh, you should take this class." And it was like a solo one person show playwriting class, because Iowa had a bunch of theaters. So, you as a student could produce a show.

So, I started producing my shows. And then there was also kind of an open mic night thing called No Shame. So, you could write a script, like a five-minute kind of thing. And then, if there was a slot, you could perform it Friday night—a script in hand kind of thing. So, I think it was those elements that really got me more focused on writing as a whole.

I guess in my early twenties is when I really kind of more seriously considered it. And it was hard for me to use the word writer, I don't know why. But I was writing and creating and putting things up. So, it was kind of that desire to make things.

Was playwriting the path you thought at that point?

Lawrence Allan: Yeah, I think playwriting was a path for me to have something to make on the stage, be it my own particular vision of what a theater piece should be, or just an opportunity to make something with my friends. But yeah, I think for the longest time. It's only within the past 10 years that I've kind of pushed playwriting away.

So, it was the path for a very long time, as far as like being a theater artist, as a theater maker. You know: having a script and then putting it up and creating something or having someone else produce it and things like that, but being involved.

So ultimately after a few years —after Iowa—I was a few years in Minneapolis. I was improvising and self-producing there.

Then I did graduate school and playwriting at the University of Texas at Austin. And then to New York to have a rearing career —a roaring career?—in playwriting in New York, which didn't quite happen. But that's all right.

How much was acting a part of that?

Lawrence Allan: It became less and less. Certainly, all through undergraduate, I was acting as well as writing and directing. I mean, I never acted in any of the things that I wrote, except for the No Shame stuff, which is, you know, barely rehearsed. So, acting was in parallel with writing and directing.

I did eventually do solo work as a writer that I wrote in Minneapolis, but I had someone else direct that. So, in some ways they went hand in hand. I mean, definitely my experience as an actor influenced the writing, in a sense of what—as an actor—I wanted from a script or I needed from a script, to launch my imagination as an actor. So, they definitely went hand in hand.

How did improvisation help you as a writer?

Lawrence Allan: That's a great question because I feel like it's only recently that I would have a good answer to that. I think as a writer, I've never been super excited of outlining. So, I'm definitely a discovery writer. Now I know enough of dramatic structure and stuff like that to kind of be on the lookout for moments or head towards a moment.

But I think improvisation gave me the confidence that—if I trust myself and trust my partners, if we're talking just pure improv—that I can step onto the stage and because we've made agreements and we're going to Yes, And, and blah, blah, blah, and really listen, then it's going to work out. Something's going to happen, because we're in touch with our own little lizard brains or whatever. Something is going to happen and it will be okay.

And it's that tension of potential failure that—I've realized only in the past couple of years—I kind of need that tension of failure and I don't know exactly what I'm doing, in order for me to really be motivated to sit down and plow ahead.

But it also, arguably, makes things less precious to me. Because with improv, it's a glorious 10 or 15 minutes and then it's gone. Yes, you could write it all down, but there's just something about the moment of it being created in front of you that has an extra power that rehearsed doesn't have. I'm not saying rehearsed stuff is bad, but an audience watching somebody create a song out of nowhere—it's fantastic. But if they were to do that song again, it's probably not going to be the best song. So, you're not precious.

I shocked somebody at a conference recently and was like, "Oh yeah, I just deleted 20 pages." It's like, "What?" I'm like, "Yeah, I don't mind." If I'm heading off somewhere and it doesn't work out, I can delete it. Maybe I'll save a line or two. Because I know it's the thing that is more important than time or work or whatever.

And that's something you wouldn't have learned if you hadn't had that improv training.

Lawrence Allan: Yeah, yeah, yeah. But it also took me 15 years after that improv training to see how it connected to my writing in a very specific way. But I've always been that way as a writer. I always hated myself for it. I could do an outline if I need to, but I feel if I'm working off of an outline, it's harder for me to be excited about it. Because I feel like the challenge of the creative work has already been done for me.

I get why some people really love that, because it's like, "Okay, I just have to figure out what they say. I don't have to figure out the plot." But the whole tapestry is what's exciting to me. So, it's harder for me to sit with an outline and be excited.

I've only read one of the two books, but it does have an improvisational feel to it. You can't really anticipate what's going to happen next.

Lawrence Allan: And what I love with good improv is when a scene is starting and it's working, it's working. And then somehow when something just comes together like at the end of the scene or like if it's a series of scenes that everything just comes together just magically.

And, for the performers and for the audience, it's this lovely moment of just, "Oh, we've all arrived here. We don't know how we got here, but this is like a fantastic culmination of this story-line of a muffin shop owner who meets a Martian. And they go on to take over the world." It's just very satisfying when those moments happen.

So, it sounds like you were the cliche of the struggling play-wright in New York. Is that kind of accurate?

Lawrence Allan: Yeah.

You weren't a cliche. You're Larry. Larry's not a cliche.

Lawrence Allan: I was the biggest cliche ever. No. I mean, it's tough. It's a tough business to get into. It can be really reward-ing, emotionally, but it's tough. The business of playwriting. It's not like *Iron Man* movie expensive to put on a play, but when they tried to make the *Spider Man* musical, that was tens of millions of dollars. How are you ever going to make that money back? So, I was a struggling playwright or trying to find my place in New York City.

But then—my wife is Indian—and she had started working with a woman who was Pakistani in New York who made, basically soap opera TV shows for consumption back in Pakistan. And she asked if I'd be interested in writing some episodes. She was doing kind of an anthology series of South Asians in New York City. She asked if I had some ideas, if I'd be interested. And I said, "Well..." And she said, "I'll pay you." And I said, "Okay."

Suddenly you're interested.

Lawrence Allan: Suddenly. Yeah. Suddenly I have ideas. And so, I wrote a few episodes for that. And I thought, "Oh, that was fun." So, I wrote what the first series—15 episodes—by myself. and it was great. I had to turn out a lot of pages in a day. But what convinced me to abandon playwriting—or at least move away from it—was in this TV show, people were getting killed off one by one. And I was running out of ways of killing people off, because I was getting punchy by the end of the whole process.

So, I'm like, "All right, well someone's gonna get blown up in a car." So. it's super low budget. I didn't know how they're going to blow up a car. I couldn't care less at that point. I was too tired.

And then I saw the trailer. They put out a trailer for it. And this was their first murder mystery TV show, they'd never done a murder thriller before on Pakistani TV. And I'm watching the trailer, like, "Oh, that's kind of interesting." "Ooh, it's kind of creepy, but it's, you know, low budget." And then, they get to this car, and it explodes. I'm like, "Oh my God, they blew up a car for me." I mean, I don't know how, I've never actually seen all of the show. I've seen like 45 seconds of a scene from the show.

But you wrote in a script "car blows up," and you looked at the screen and the car blew up

Lawrence Allan: Blew up. And I'm like, "This is awesome." So, I started more seriously considering moving into TV, and to a degree, film. This would have been, let's see, 2007 or so. And this was when a lot of playwrights were moving into television. I feel it's not as much anymore. I feel the studios aren't rushing to find a playwright to run a TV show or staff on a TV show as much anymore. But there was a big rush of playwrights into television.

So, I started doing the classes and writing the pilots. And then eventually I somehow convinced my wife—who's also an actor —let's move to LA. Because I want to move into there and all production is really based out here in LA. So, this was only the real logical choice to move to.

So then, soon after that I got my first manager. And soon after that I fired my first manager and got my second manager and started writing the pilots, going on meetings, having good meetings. I mean, a good meeting is like, "Hey, next time you have another script, reach out to us. "Okay, you're not buying this one? All right."

And you worked on a lot of pilots at that point, right?

Lawrence Allan: That became the new model of the business —I wouldn't be able to pinpoint when that started, that was before my time of pursuing it—because in the eighties and nineties and before that, you would write a spec of an existing show to show that you could write television.

I mean, your first job is always going to be as a staff writer. Unless it's an extraordinary situation, you're going to be a staff writer on someone else's show, and you'll have to write in their voice. So, it used to be you would write a spec of your *seaQuest DSV* or whatever it was called. Or *MASH* and stuff like that.

But somewhere—I think in the late nineties, early two thousands—it started changing that they wanted original things, because they wanted to hear your voice. But it was also an opportunity for, "Oh, maybe this pilot can sell." So, it became an opportunity for managements and agents to maybe sell a script as well as sell their writer.

So, only for competitions did I ever write any spec scripts for any existing shows. Primarily, the business was write an original pilot. Hopefully it's a good pilot that introduces the characters ... introduces what the story is going to be for the overall series ... and what's the story of this particular episode.

Let's just quickly recap. You've got acting experience. You've got improv experience. You've got playwriting experience. You're one of the top Pakistani TV writers—

Lawrence Allan: Yeah.

At that point, you've written a bunch of pilots. You've got your feet really, I would say pretty well wet in the Hollywood system. You're taking meetings. And then you decide to write a novel. Where did that come from?

Lawrence Allan: So, it goes back to the *Big Fat Fuck-Up* pilot. I know for a period that's what I was calling it. But I think I was calling it *Public Eye* for a while. I was being very network friendly. So, I remember—because I love, I love that pilot and I love Jimmy Cooper, the main character—and I remember I was in a meeting with a former producer of *Ally McBeal*.

It was one of my last meetings I had on this particular pilot. So, I had this meeting with this guy. He was everything you want from an *Ally McBeal* producer; he had this great purple sweater and was well dressed and, you know, just like clearly a very successful producer. And I remember in the meeting, he was like, "Oh, this is great. This pilot's great. It shows that you could really do this job." And in my head, I'm like, "So, are you going to hire me?" And there was no hiring.

But I remember saying to him, "Well, listen, I love this script. And if no one ever buys it, I'm turning it into a book. And then you'll pay more for it later." And he was like, "Ha ha ha."

But in the back of my head, I'm already kind of thinking. And I had started dabbling a little bit in prose. Not since high school had I really written much prose, but I started dabbling in again. Just to have writing for myself. It was right before the pandemic. There was the California Crime Writers Conference, and I don't know why I decided to go, but I decided to go. And I had some pages of the book and I paid for one of those, you know, have an agent or editor read the first five pages and give you feedback. Again, I don't know why I did that. Maybe I just was looking for someone to say I'm good or something or whatever.

And I distinctly remember the meeting, because she started off with, "Well, this is going to be short." And she knows what that effect is. It's going to be like, "Oh God, is it that bad?" And she said, "I love it. I want to see the whole thing. Do you have any questions?"

So, I guess my first five pages were really good. And so, we just talked about the business. And I mean, I had to admit to her, I don't have the full book yet. I've still got to finish it. But I know where it's heading, because I had the pilot to base stuff on. So that was great. That gave me the encouragement to really finish it.

And so, I worked with a developmental editor, because I think I needed someone to kind of hold my hand a little bit. Because, as I've said in other interviews, writing a script is like writing a haiku. If it's a pilot script, you've got about 60 pages, don't go much more than that. Whereas a novel is like writing a novel. You've got all this space. So, I was freaked out a little bit. So, I wrote it. I sent it off to her. She passed on it. I pouted a few days. And then decided, "Well, okay, I'll keep pursuing other agents." And then that's when the pandemic started.

Ultimately, I'm independently or self-published, whichever terminology you want to use. I'm doing that because I realized during the pandemic—and I was getting fine feedback from agents, but no one wanted the book or to sign me—and that's fine. But then I decided, okay, well, I remember that some of the happiest periods of my artistic life was when I was self-producing my plays in Minneapolis. I would write a script, I cast my friends or cast some people and I'd build a set or build the props or whatever. And it would be exactly like the strange quirky imagination that I have sometimes.

I still look back upon that as that was great fun. Now, maybe I wasn't as good as a businessperson. I didn't translate that into the playwriting career, but it was the most fun. So, I realized, "Oh, I could do that as a novelist." The technology is advanced now that I don't have to sign away and print up 10,000 copies of the book and mail it out. I don't have to do that.

And so, I set out to do that. I hired a good editor. I hired a good cover artist, and I really focused on making the best book I could.

So that happened during the pandemic, but also what happened during the pandemic was I realized I didn't want to pursue TV anymore. That I was so exhausted by that process of write a pilot, have meetings, write another pilot, have meetings.

I was just so burnt out. So, I was quitting one thing and then investing in something else, because by that point, prose writing had become fun writing for me, where the TV thing was just such a drag on my soul for me personally. Other people might still enjoy it.

It was something that was fun to do and it was solely mine. I could write the book how I wanted it to be. I could do all of that stuff. So, it became very much an empowerment kind of thing as an artist, like I'm doing it this way and I'm very happy to do it.

So, I guess that ultimately a pandemic was good for me. It made me realize I could have fun writing and creating as a novelist. And it's been great, the feedback has been really wonderful. When someone just emails me and says, "Oh, I just finished the book. It was great."

That's the best thing in the world.

Lawrence Allan: It really is.

It really is. So, before we dive into how your playwriting and screenwriting helped inform your writing in the prose world, I got to ask you: The title. Are you happy about that? Was that a good decision? Would you still do it?

Lawrence Allan: I would. Maybe. Because yes, it limits me. I can't do Amazon sponsored ads. I could still do Facebook ads. Now, obviously I'd rather do Amazon ads, because that's where people are shopping for books.

I don't know where I came up with the title for the first book. But it just filled me with such glee. And the title of the second book, just the whole naming system of it kind of filled me with such glee.

I remember at this year's Bouchercon, I was talking with an author and she was talking with another author and she told him about my book and told the title. And just his reaction to the title. There's something about it. I mean, it's a transgressive title. My titles are transgressive, but they're not transgressive in a terrible, you know, jokey way.

I knew at some point I would face consequences for the title of my books. I just expected different consequences. I just expected, well, Walmart will never stock my book, but I can still sell it on Amazon.

And there's also a certain amount of glee I get at award shows when clearly the emcee, they're going along and they hadn't made a choice of what to do with my book title until they get to it. So, there's always "Hound of Baskervilles by Cartho Cornadora," and then "Big Fat ... F ... Up by Lawrence..." So, you can see that moment: are you going to say it? What are you going to do? You know, or Big Effing deal or whatever.

I remember years ago—right around the time the first book came out—when someone on one of the groups was asking, "Oh, I'm doing a book signing. Anybody want to join me?" And I said, "Oh, I'd love to." And I sent her the title of my book, but you know, it's the F and then like the curly @ exclamation K U P. And she emailed me right back and said, "How do you pronounce that?" So, I had to email her back and say, "Exactly how it sounds."

And then she said, "I don't think the bookstore owner would like to do that." And then I had the audacity to look up her book. And there's a beheading in it. My book is, save for the language, is pretty PG, PG-13. It's definitely not dark. There are network television levels of sex, it's not bloody and gory. The most transgressive thing is the title.

And so, to me, this is my bouncer. If you don't appreciate the joke of this title, if you're not leaning in because of the title, then just don't come in. Because there's other things that are kind of making fun of titles and mysteries and all that stuff in the books too.

The audience self-selects.

Lawrence Allan: An audience self-selects. Yeah. So, I don't regret it because there's just too much leaning in and the covers are so great. It's fine. I'm not going to necessarily be a *New York Times* bestseller, but that's okay. I wouldn't mind it, but I'm not pursuing it. That's not my goal.

So, how did your experience in screenwriting and play-writing prepare you for writing that first novel?

Lawrence Allan: That's a good question. I think two things come to my mind. I think one is dialogue, because that's really the meat of a script is the dialogue. A screenplay or a TV script is going to basically have action lines and dialogue. That's basically it. You don't get anything more. And so, I think writing a lot of dialogue, I think, helped me come to write dialogue in prose. I don't think my scenes go on too long,

You know when to get in, you know when to get out, you understand pace.

Lawrence Allan: Yeah. There are no long monologues in my books. Because it would be incredibly rare to have a long monologue in a TV show. So, that's probably just habit.

I think, the quality of my dialogue in my books is really good because for 20-some years, that was the main cudgel of telling a story—dialogue.

And I also think clarity of action on the page. Because when you're writing a script, that script is going to go to a bunch of people. And so, it needs things to be absolutely clear what's happening. And I don't mean action, like "he walked across the room, he picked up his coffee mug." That kind of stuff, you're not necessarily going to put in. But if it's an action sequence—it's a car chase or a foot chase through a hospital—you need to really make those moments very clear on the page, so someone's reading it, they can easily imagine it.

Because you don't want *any* confusion. You don't want them to have to work hard (and not because executives are lazy, or their assistants are lazy). But they're reading so many scripts that if there's for any reason, they're like, "I don't understand what's happening," they will put it aside. They are looking for reasons to not have to finish your script, because they go home every weekend with piles of scripts.

I would suggest readers look at the opening of your first Jimmy Cooper book, which opens with a chase scene. Which is completely clear as to what's happening throughout. And that's not only a testament to your screenwriting, but if you had a scene that was confusing that opens your book, people aren't going to keep reading it. Just like they're not going to keep reading it in screenplay form.

Yet you have a chase scene where we always know where we are and what direction we're headed and what the stakes are at every moment. And I think that's something that you got from screenwriting.

Lawrence Allan: Yeah. I mean, that opening chase was in the original pilot. I always worked hard at making it clear. And that might mean in the scripts and definitely in my books, I don't mind short paragraphs. You have a long paragraph and people are going to read the first line, skim, and read the end.

So, if it's really important, like, "He throws a punch, and it connected," maybe that's one paragraph. And then the next paragraph is the reaction by the other person. Or something like that. Rather than compressing it.

In a script, there's always a lot of white space. I would encourage writers—prose writers who are interested in this— not to watch the movies, but to read the scripts and see how the scripts are functioning.

Because you're exactly right: it's got to be clear, because all action scenes really do need to tell a story. They can't just be action for action's sake. They need to tell almost a beginning, middle and end, just like a movie as a whole. Each scene is doing that. So, each action scene has a clear beginning, middle and end.

And you also need a sense of clarity from the production stand-point. They need to know like, "Oh, we're going to be on a high-way. So, we have to find a highway. Oh, there's five cars in this thing. There's this, this, this, and this." That might all change in pre-production, but they get a sense of how much is this movie going to cost us? What is happening?

But just from a storytelling perspective, in moviemaking they want to be captivated at the script level. So as the writer, they have to be incredibly clear with the action scenes, if it's an action movie. Or even if it's not an action movie, you're still not going to find paragraphs of "He sat in this chair and blah, blah, blah." Within a scene or two, there might be some action moments, but those are all going to be in service of character, in service of the emotional moment of that scene.

Talking about this with my wife—because actors are also looking at this—actors are looking for clues in the dialogue and what action there might be to create a whole character. So, you as a writer need to make specific choices, like how will a character talk? What actions are important to the character? Do they bring snacks to board meetings?

So, the two big things that kind of go back to the original question are dialogue and clarity of action on the page.

And like you said, they're always looking for a reason to say no. And so, it has to be beyond that opening chase scene. You've got to do that all the way to the end credits.

Lawrence Allan: Yeah. Well, I mean, it's funny because we talk about, there'll be at conferences, they'll talk about that opening line to get people to buy the book. But what about the line that makes them turn the page? You have to have that exciting opening, but you also have to keep your reader engaged. But at the same time, it's not just about action, action, action, because then that would be boring. So, you just kind of find the musicality of your own work.

Did the work you did in playwriting and screenwriting help you in streamlining and hiding exposition.

Lawrence Allan: Yes, yes. I did a class with a writer named Corey Mandell, who I believe is still teaching and maybe teaching online. I learned so many fabulous things from him. I remember one night I came home, and I said to my wife: "I learned so much today. I learned more today than in three years of my master's playwriting program."

He had a great idea about exposition. I actually prefer to use the word context than exposition, because I think exposition is so weighted. "Oh, we hate exposition."

But we need exposition. We need the context of why is this important? So, I like using the word context, because it makes me happier. I don't know.

Corey said, "Oh, you can do exposition, but if the characters are in conflict, it won't feel like an information dump." And he showed us a clip from *Tootsie*. I feel like it's at the very beginning of the movie, where he's talking with his agent. And there's so much information in that scene about what kind of person Dustin Hoffman's character is, what he wants, all of this stuff. If Dustin Hoffman's character just delivered it over coffee to a best friend, we'd be like, "Well, here's the exposition." But because it's in conflict with two characters, we're absorbing the information, we're absorbing the context, but we're not thinking about it as information.

And I can point to a scene in my first book. I feel like it's Chapter Five or Six. But it's the scene after he gets the client, Alicia, and she's a very Paris Hilton kind of character. And not the kind of client that Jimmy's mom who runs the law firm wants. She is awfully clownish.

And so, Greta, his mom is really pissed off. And there's a scene between Greta, Jimmy and his sister, Erica, about, "What the fuck is this nonsense?" And there's a lot of exposition being dropped in that conversation: You understand how these characters relate to each other, you understand what they need, you understand some of their history. But we don't care, we're not unhappy with it, because it's in conflict, and we're feeling our way into this family dynamic. We're witnessing it, not sitting back and having information dumped on us.

I've used the *Tootsie* scene for years as the best example of how much information we've learned in this two-and-a-half-minute piece. It's an excellent scene. So overall, is there a principle that you've taken from your playwriting and screenwriting and putting it into novel writing? You just wouldn't have been able to do that if you hadn't had that

playwriting, screenwriting experience? I think I know what yours is, but I want you to decide yourself.

Lawrence Allan: Oh, oh, great. I'd love to hear it. That's a good question. I think it's definitely, get in and get out. That is a big one. I might add, just don't be boring. Keep an audience engaged and guessing. Maybe that's it?

I think it is, and I think you got that from improv. I think you took everything you learned up to that point, and then when you're on stage in front of an audience, you have to keep that energy going. I think you found a way to take that and put that on the page.

Lawrence Allan: I'm always fascinated by people who are really intimidated by improv. I mean, it's a muscle. It's a muscle you learn and it's a muscle you practice. But I love that feeling of, I don't know what's going to happen, but as long as I'm kind of present and my partners are present, it's going to be fine.

The scene might not be great. Someone will cut it and then we'll move on to something else. But when it works, it's just this magical, magical thing.

And I think you also learned your ability to edit and to throw stuff out, which is a very hard thing to learn.

Lawrence Allan: Yeah. I think, improv and doing No Shame are the two biggest. Because No Shame was once a week, so you could perform or not perform. I generally wanted to do something. So, once a week, I'm writing something new. And it might work. It might not work. I had so many terrible moments that some of my friends and I still joke about, "Oh, remember that one? Ha ha ha."

But none of it became precious. I mean, the work is important, but it wasn't precious. I don't have a file. I know some writers are like, "Oh, I love that scene. And so, it's pasted it into this big ongoing file." I might have a scene that I love, but then I'll just remember it. It's like, "Oh, that was a great scene." So, the editing is a really important thing, I think.

So, final question for you: For aspiring novelists, what one piece of advice would you give them based on your experience in screenwriting and playwriting?

Lawrence Allan: The advice I always give in general is finish something. Just finish it. Because you can't make anything better if there's no *thing* to make. So, you have to get to the end.

I would also say, just in the context of this particular conversation, I would recommend if you feel like you want to be better at dialogue, then I would say go read scripts. I mean, you can consume the movies, but you're going to see those movies through the filter of, hopefully, a great actor. But if you read the scripts, you're kind of seeing where those great actors are getting their rhythms and intonations and all of that stuff. And so, read scripts.

But my overall advice would just always be, you have to finish the thing. You can't edit anything unless it's there.

APRIL SMITH

April Smith has paid some serious dues when it comes to writing for both TV and novels. She started off getting creative writing degrees from a couple big name schools—Boston University and Stanford. After some early gigs winning awards for her copywriting at an ad agency, she made the leap to Hollywood.

Smith wrote for many hit TV shows that are probably very familiar —Friends, Lou Grant, Cagney & Lacey, Chicago Hope. Her television writing chops earned her three Emmy nominations, including one for the Ernie Kovacs biopic she did in 1984. Her adaptation skills even stretched to bringing Stephen King's stories to life for the Nightmares & Dreamscapes anthology series.

But Smith has also made her mark as a novelist. She's the author of several novels—with major publishers like Knopf and Vintage behind her. She is best known for her mystery/thriller series centered around FBI Agent Ana Grey, but she's also drawn acclaim for her forays into historical fiction.

As the following interview makes clear, Smith's years grinding it out in TV writers' rooms really drilled into her the importance of full immersion into research for her novels. Her dedication to grounding every story in exhaustive factual details is what allows her fiction to feel authentic and real. It's a skill she honed doing all that writers' room work that prized—and rewarded—getting the facts right.

I'm looking at your CV: Undergraduate Creative Writing, Graduate Creative Writing. I'm guessing the plan was always some form of writing. Is that right?

April Smith: Yes. If I had a plan, but yes. I mean, I always wrote. I wrote from the time I could think or write or anything. I was submitting articles to *American Girl* magazine back in the day. It just is always with me.

Is it a family thing or were you the outlier?

April Smith: No, actually, that's a question that cuts to the heart of it. My dad, Dr. Philip Smith, was an avid reader. And I was inspired by his collection of sci-fi paperbacks, mainly by their covers. But he was, I guess what you'd call an amateur writer.

He did publish one story in a science fiction magazine. He was a general practitioner doctor in the Bronx. And so, he published this one story about a doctor who could cure everybody and everything. And so, people came from miles. And in the end, the doctor cuts his own throat. *[LAUGHS]* So that's what I grew up with, you know, way out there.

And he had this practice in the Bronx, but he would come home in the afternoons for this early dinner. And so, he would just tell me stories and jokes. And he would sit at the dining room table and type on his Red Royal typewriter. So, it was part of normal life for me, to be with someone who was that strange. That did that and had these crazy ambitions.

But you also saw someone write. It wasn't mysterious. You saw someone do it and he got published. I don't know if you ever went into therapy and brought that story in with you and handed it to the therapist.

April Smith: Probably.

"What do you make of this?" So, you get a bachelor's degree and a graduate degree in creative writing. And you said there wasn't much of a plan, but you ended up in advertising and copywriting.

April Smith: Okay. Well, to back up just a slight bit, there was a plan at Stanford to be a real writer. Like those before us. And we're very serious there about creative writing and how to structure stories and honesty and craft. Craft was really important. Scott Turow was in my class, for example. It was serious.

And out of that, I published my first short story in the *Atlantic*. Tilly Olsen was running the seminar on my year. And so, you can imagine how serious it was. So, I wrote this story called *Sailing*. I thought, "Okay, here's a story." And then she said, "No, you have to send this somewhere."

So, I had been living in Boston, etc. Anyway, I sent it to the *Atlantic* and they published it. And that was a thrill because we were all graduate students with no money. And then somebody wrote, "Oh, oh boy, everybody here likes this story, *Sailing*." And this check fell out. It was like probably for $300 or something, but it made it so I could stay there and continue to write. So that was the first kind of indication that I was on the right path.

I've got to back up here. Was your dad still around at that point?

April Smith: He was.

What did he think about you getting published in *The Atlantic*?

April Smith: He was thrilled. This story, *Sailing*, was about our family on this sailboat, which was real, and it was a slightly dysfunctional family. So, he had it both ways. No, he was proud. Very proud.

And in your story, the father didn't slit his throat at the end of the story?

April Smith: No, he didn't. *[LAUGHS]* No, because my mother was sailing the ship.

All right, so you go into therapy with both those stories and get a lot to work with. So that was a very good start as a writer. What happened then?

April Smith: Well, then you had to make a living. So, I ended up leaving California, went back to Boston and worked for an ad agency. Writing copy and producing radio commercials. But I had an agent who represented a lot of the people on my seminar. So that was already starting to build the structure for being a real writer.

And so, I went back to Boston. But while I was working, I was working on a novel that never got published. And it was just part of my habit to be writing every day. And then, well, then I came out to Hollywood. My dear friend Dan Wakefield sold a TV show called *James at 16*. To make a long story short, he got zipped out to Hollywood to produce this show.

He was all high as a kite, I mean, emotionally. At the Chateau Marmont, LA, the whole thing. And he said to me, "You gotta come out to LA."

I mean, here I am in Cambridge, I have a nice apartment, blah, blah. So, I went out there on a lark, really, and stayed at the

Chateau. He put me up. He was kind. And for some reason, I had a meeting that morning with the head of TV at Fox, which he had arranged. And I'm sitting in this huge office on the Fox lot, and the executive, David Sontag said, "So have you ever written for television?" "No." "Well, what have you written?"

And I told him about this short story, *Sailing*. It was published in *The Atlantic*. And he was looking for a show. And so, I pitched him the idea of a boy who goes in a sailboat around the world. His parents die, he goes in the sailboat.

And I never went back. I mean, I never went back to Cambridge. I had a friend drive my car out and I just started hanging out on the Fox lot. I stayed in the marina in one of those temporary apartments. And just stayed here. And started getting gigs in Hollywood. I got an agent, Dan introduced me to his agent. And I went from there and kind of never stopped writing for Hollywood.

You really have never stopped. It's really impressive. Your IMDB, it's such a variety of things from comedy to drama to biopic. It's just amazing.

April Smith: Thank you. Yeah, I was definitely on a roll. But don't forget, this was network television, and a lot of original dramas were being produced. We had movies of the week, for example, a great genre for me. I wrote a lot of them. And so, it was an open market. And I had this wonderful man who's still a very dear friend, Dan, as an anchor. So, I was really lucky.

Before we dig into novel writing, I have a couple questions concerning some of the stuff you wrote for TV, just because I'm curious. I see you have a credit on *Friends*. Were you on staff at *Friends*?

April Smith: No, that was just a freelance script. That was one of my first.

So, have you had experience in a writer's room? Or are you generally just writing on your own?

April Smith: I learned how to be in the room when I got hired on *Lou Grant.*

What did you learn in order to be in the room? What does it take to be in the room?

April Smith: Well, first of all, it takes a leader. Gene Reynolds was the leader, you know him, right? A million Emmys. He and Alan Burns were the anchors, and they had a method of how you break down stories. And it was very inclusive. We did it all together. There were like four writers in the room.

And so, we had this big white board. This was his method. And as we would break down stories, you'd write ideas: Lou goes to the bathroom, the pipes are broken, he has to go to his neighbor, that kind of thing. Just spit balling. But it was communal.

We did not have computers. In fact, one of my first jobs there as story editor was at the end of this process, putting all these notes together and literally typing them. Typing them. And handing it to a messenger who would show up at the gate. Giving him the actual paper typed. And then he would take it and get it Xeroxed. So, it was very crafty. Hands on.

But I learned. I'm a team player and this was a beautiful team of talented writers. And because Gene was such a strong leader, we got it done without a lot of mess and ego going on. And he handled the actors, and he had control of the network. He was just brilliant. Brilliant.

So, you had the security of knowing that whatever went on, you know, creatively: A., it had a purpose; B., it would be used somehow; and C., it was protected. We were protected from the network.

Right, but how great to have that. I've heard horror stories about rooms that didn't have leaders like that. And I've heard horror stories about rooms that went on all night. And they didn't have any concern for your family life, for your actual health, and it was all top down. And it sounds like with those guys, you really got into a great learning situation.

April Smith: I did. I did. So, when I ran the room, as it were, for *Cagney and Lacey,* I took those principals with me. I hired the staff, which was three other guys, but they were all really talented. I read piles of scripts, but I was looking for talent and I found it.

And so, we did the same thing. I mean, I think this was new to them, but we had the whiteboard, we had the open conversations, we had the secretary taking down the notes, and then producing the scripts. And it went pretty smoothly.

And it was enormous pressure, because they had nothing. They got picked up. They didn't have typewriters. They didn't have an office. They didn't know what the hell they were doing. And Robert Crais and I went to New York to research the New York City Police Department. And that was crucial, because in general, I write reality-based stories. And I need those details. So, Bob and I went to New York, and we were taken around by NYPD and we went to crime scenes and, you know, the whole thing.

So that gave us a grounding and emotional connection, as well as details, to the world that we were creating. So, this wasn't just making it up. I think that's one thing that is true through all my work, is that there's a grounding in a kind of reality going in.

You guys were doing 22, 24 episodes a year with that small four or five group of writers?

April Smith: Yeah.

Wow. That's a lot of work.

April Smith: It's a lot of work.

So, before we dive into novel writing, just a couple more questions on, well first, making the leap from *Lou Grant* staff writer, to showrunner on *Cagney and Lacey*. How did that happen?

April Smith: Well, first of all, *Lou Grant* was canceled. That was the big initiating force here. *Lou Grant* was cancelled, and so everybody was let loose. And my husband and I were going to actually go to the islands for a vacation when I got this call that Barney Rosenzweig wanted to meet with me. And how that happened, I'm not really sure. Probably through my agents. But so, we turned around and came back to L.A., because it's what I always wanted, right, was to run it.

And so, we just came back to L. A. And I walked in the room and there's Barney. And first thing he said to me is, "Wow, you're smaller than I thought you would be." And the second thing he said to me was, quote, "Lincoln freed the slaves, but I've got you." [LONG PAUSE] Yeah. Kind of a difference.

Yeah, that's not the same room that you just came out of.

April Smith: Exactly. Exactly.

So, what do you do to survive in that, then? Because you obviously thrived in it.

April Smith: Well, by hiring good people. By hiring real writers. But we knew what we were doing, and we did it, and the network appreciated it. And it became a hit.

One more TV question, and then we're going to talk about novels. I've not had a chance to talk to someone who's adapted Stephen King. What was that process like?

April Smith: Well, it was... fantastic. First of all, you know, it was Stephen King's short stories, *Nightmares and Dreamscapes*. So it was, I don't know how many, maybe eight separate stories that were taken, six or eight.

And it was all shot in Australia, and Bill Haber was in charge, and he was just fantastic. Hired only the best directors. And I mean, adapting Stephen King is really challenging, because there are things you can do in prose that it's very hard to translate literally to the screen. There are lots of leaps in there. But it was a peak experience.

I never had any contact actually with him, but I heard that he liked the scripts. I mean, it was challenging. Like, okay, *Umney's Last Case* was about a writer, a sort of pulp detective writer, who is at his typewriter every day. He has a character. And then one day he switches places with his own character.

Okay, so this writer from our time ends up, I think he comes popping up in a swimming pool in 1941 Los Angeles, and stuff happens. William Macy played both roles, which was—gives me the chills just remembering that. We wanted that to be a series, but he didn't want to do that.

And then the other one was a classic. I think Hitchcock did something like this. It was called *Autopsy Room Four*. And it's a guy who's in an autopsy room, but he's not dead.

That would come under the nightmare scenario, as opposed to being a dreamscape.

April Smith: And he can't speak, and they're about to cut him open.

Like a locked in syndrome sort of thing?

April Smith: Yeah, right. I mean, it's a great series, I gotta say. It should have gotten more attention. It was TNT.

So, you've gone back and forth writing TV, writing novels. If I got the chronology right, the first Ana Grey novel was the first one. What was it that inspired that move? Because you were writing and you're getting paid for it. Why add novels to your list of things you're doing?

April Smith: Well, because... of two things.

One was the writer's strike of 1988. And the second thing was a story that had been told to me. My kids were really young at the time, and so there were these parallel worlds of the moms and the nannies, so called. And a story was told to me by one of the moms about—nanny is probably not the right word, but housekeeper/nanny. But anyway, she was in charge of this affluent woman's kids. And she suddenly got fired and there were two societies: the white moms, the Hispanic caretakers. So, through the network of the Hispanic caretakers, my hired wonderful person told me the story that the lady fired her housekeeper because she'd found out that the lady had had an affair and was paranoid and fired her.

But the whole societal segregation of these two cultures that are side by side and so intimate, was fascinating and it had not been dramatized or explored really. The way these two currents work in daily life. And so—it just I'm getting the chills thinking about it. One thing I know, this is a story. You know, the story meter goes off.

And so, I took that and wrote *North of Montana*, my first novel of suspense. And it culturally was sort of ahead of its time, because I created an FBI agent, Ana Grey, who is half Hispanic and half white, but doesn't know that she has Hispanic heritage. So, you have all these parallel stories of discovery and retribution going on. And I just wrote that on spec.

Just because it came to you and you wanted to do it?

April Smith: Yeah. And I wasn't working.

Right, because of the strike. You said something interesting there. You said you knew immediately it was a story. Was that a muscle that you picked up in the *Lou Grant* and the *Cagney and Lacey* room, where you could tell immediately what was going to work and what wasn't going to work as a story?

April Smith: Yes, I think for sure that sixth sense was honed there. But don't forget, I'd been in these really privileged situations with real writers, like at Stanford, with Scott Turow and others, where we would sit around in a big room and people would read their work. So, the nuts and bolts of how these things are put together and what inspires you was a daily conversation. So, it wasn't like I'd never talked to other writers before. I mean, I learned their tricks of the trade.

So, was there anything you brought to that first novel that you can kind of look back on and say, "I was able to do that as well as I did it because of doing *Lou Grant* for all those years and all those episodes and doing *Cagney and Lacey*" all that time? Was there something in particular you think helped you do that?

April Smith: Well, one thing was the research. I mean, on *Lou Grant*, we were research addicted. I mean, we didn't do anything without going into the field, or at least certainly validating what we did a million ways from one.

So, my first move was to align myself with the FBI, because she's an FBI agent. And I did that and, you know, people want you to write their stories. And I had come with some cachet and I think I came in through the publicist. I'm not sure. But I did connect with the FBI publicist. And then, because I was writing about a Hispanic woman—an FBI agent—I mean, she's biracial. And I sort of worked that angle and got hooked up with Hispanic women FBI agents.

And to make a long story short, I really became embedded with the FBI in Los Angeles. And that was just a treasure.

I imagine you're still using things in your novels from that first being embedded, you get so much information.

April Smith: For sure. I mean, it was great because you had access through the bureau to police departments. You know, it's all a brother and sisterhood. And it was beautiful, actually. So, it enabled me to write *North of Montana*.

And again, there wasn't any time limit. We were on strike, so I could do it as long as possible. And they had respect for *Lou Grant*. You know, I wasn't coming from a quiz show. They had respect for the way we represented people of color and different points of view. So, I had help going in.

Were there any other specific screenwriting techniques you think you had honed that helped you on that first and then subsequent novels? Things that made it a little bit easier for you to tackle a project like that?

April Smith: Well, yeah, I just did the same thing we did in the room. I had the whiteboard. And was just writing down random ideas and then typing them. And just going through that process over and over and over. So, yeah, the stuff that Gene Reynolds taught us has helped. It taught me how.

One of the things you had to deal with at that time in TV were act breaks, which we still run into from time to time now, but not as often. It's that sort of cliffhanger thing that I think makes screenwriters who become novelists better at keeping the pace going.

Were you finding that you're bringing that sort of thinking with you when you wrote, trying to create those moments of, "I want you to turn the page, I want you to turn the page"?

April Smith: Yeah, very much so. That's a really good question that goes to the heart of it. Absolutely. It becomes a rhythm, and you know when it's not working. Because, yes, they have to turn the page.

Did you have any tricks when you guys were doing *Lou Grant* or *Cagney and Lacey* of how to make that happen organically, so it didn't seem like you were forcing an act break?

April Smith: Well, it all has to do with the story you're telling. It's not that hard once you know what the story is, where to pause it. It comes pretty naturally. I mean, sometimes you move them around a lot. But you know when there's an end of an exhale or a pause. It's intuitive.

Would that sort of thing likely be even mapped out on the whiteboard, where you'd know here's the end of Act One, here's the beginning?

April Smith: Oh, yeah. That's exactly what you would do. And then you get to draw a big line under it. [LAUGHS]

And then you order lunch.

April Smith: Yeah, exactly.

What did you learn about rewriting while you were in a screenwriting and TV writing situation that's helped you as a novelist?

April Smith: Well, it's made me realize it's necessary. Although rewriting in those days had to do with dealing with the network a lot. And that was just a fight all the time. But Gene took it, not us, on *Lou Grant*. And on *Cagney and Lacey*, I guess I took that fight.

But it's art versus commerce. And you just believe that you know better than they do how to tell a story. But there were so many stupid restrictions about things you could say and not say. That was just policy.

Any that you remember that strike you as memorable?

April Smith: Well, you can't say Tampax, for example. [LAUGHS]

I heard you speak about *A Star for Mrs. Blake*. And I know that you have taken that story, and—at the point of this presentation you were giving—you were looking into making it into a movie or a TV show of some kind. Has that progressed at all?

April Smith: It has not. And that was while I was at ABC Circle. We came really close, I wrote the script. But at that time they said it was too expensive. We didn't have the technology that we have now. And so, ships and sailing and Europe and all that stuff seemed out of the question. I really wish we could make that movie. It's from the heart.

But having written the book and then doing the screenplay, what made that easy? And what made that hard?

April Smith: It was a pretty smooth transition, to tell you the truth. I mean, that story, for those who don't know it, is about the Gold Star mothers who lost their sons—and it was sons— in World War I. And then were given the opportunity to go to France and visit their sons' graves by a major program of the U. S. government that I don't think has ever happened again. This was in the late 20s.

So, you had that, you had all the research: it was a story that, quote, laid itself out. And then, of course, there's a diverse group of women who go on this journey. So, it was all there. It was so rich.

It sounds like, again, your secret weapon as a writer of television and of novels, is research. And a complete willingness to immerse yourself until you find the story.

April Smith: That is true. It's the facts and the research, but it's also the tone. It's also how you're going to tell it, and from what point of view.

The hardest part sometimes is the narrative voice. If you're not writing from first person—like the Ana Grey books are all first person, told in her voice. So, when you have a situation like this with multiple characters, finding the tone took a while to do.

But I did have the diaries of the original soldier who accompanied the Gold Star mothers over there—Nicholas Hammond, whose father was one of those soldiers. So, I had his voice and his point of view that I could start with. Which I did.

One thing that people say to me a lot is—I go to a lot of writers' conventions—they say, "What do I need to do to get my novel made into a movie?" And I tell them I have no idea at all. It's a whole different world than I'm in. Do you have any advice to someone who's got their own series of novels or a standalone and they're interested in doing that? Any thoughts?

April Smith: It's always been hard. Of course, you want to get your book published in a big way. You have three or four months before and after publication to make a splash. So, I would really work hard with the publisher to try to get attention pre-publication—whatever it takes, do interviews, stand on the street corner. I mean, we don't even have bookstores anymore. It's scary.

For aspiring novelists, is there one piece of advice you'd give them based on your experience as both a screenwriter and a novelist?

April Smith: Well, the one piece of advice is keep writing. Keep writing. Make it your practice. Try to be regular. Try to create your own space that is just defended against everything else. I know it sounds really hard. But you can do that, even if you do it in small ways, whether it's going to the library to work or just closing your door to the family.

But believing in your own instincts and not judging yourself prematurely, what you do, what you get on paper. Understand it's a process that is mysterious. And it's a living process, and it's gonna keep changing and morphing. Think of it as a practice, like meditation or working out.

And the thing is—at least in writing novels—it takes a long time to even understand what you're doing or thinking. And put that in mind: it's the long-distance journey. It's not a sprint.

KEN LEVINE

Ken Levine is a highly accomplished writer, director, and producer who has had an incredibly prolific career in television comedy. He got his big break writing for the iconic sitcom MASH alongside his longtime writing partner David Isaacs. Levine and Isaacs then went on to work on numerous other hit shows like Cheers, Frasier, Wings, and more.

In addition to his extensive TV writing credits, Levine has also written feature films such as Volunteers, authored several books on the entertainment industry, and even called play-by-play for Major League Baseball teams like the Mariners and Padres for several years.

More recently, Levine published his comedic novel Must Kill TV, drawing from his five decades of experience working behind the scenes in the television business. The book is a biting satire that gets into the mind of a progressively unhinged TV executive seeking revenge.

One key takeaway from the interview is Levine's advice to deeply research and immerse yourself in any world you plan to write

about. He credits his mentor Gene Reynolds for instilling in him the
importance of authentic details and grounding the story in reality,
even when writing comedy.

Was being a writer always a goal?

Ken Levine: I don't know if it was always a goal. It was something that I always did. Honestly, I did not get a lot of encouragement in high school. I was a cartoonist. I still am. And I was a cartoonist on the school newspaper. And I said, "Well, I also want to write. Can I cover sports or do a humor column or something?"

And they said, "You're the cartoonist, just stick to cartoons." And I said, "Well, I really want to write, and if you won't let me write, then I'm going to quit the paper." And they said, "Then fine, quit the paper." So, that's how much my cartoons were even valued.

They called your bluff on that one, I guess.

Ken Levine: They called my bluff, yeah.

Just as a little tangent, just because I'm a big fan of your cartoons. Did you have a couple of cartoonist heroes when you were growing up? Guys that you looked at and went, "That's the kind of writing I want to do"?

Ken Levine: Well, my cartoonist heroes were more due to their cartooning than anything. Al Hirschfeld, who did the caricatures of *The New York Times*, was my god. And Mort Drucker would be another. Jack Davis. A lot of those *Mad* magazine guys.

Originally, I wanted to be in radio. I mean, I really loved radio. And a lot of my comic influences early on were disc jockeys: Bob and Ray and Dan Ingram and Dick Whittington. So, radio was a goal. I got out of college and became a Top 40-disc jockey.

Let me back up. When I was in college, I got a job as an intern at KMPC in L. A. They were the big, full-service radio station. They had the Angels and the Rams and the Bruins and, you know, they were big music personalities. And their afternoon drive time jock was Gary Owens, who was on *Laugh In* at the time. You know, "From beautiful downtown Burbank."

And I would write comedy material for Gary, for him to use on the air. I never charged him for it. I mean, I was just so thrilled that someone of the caliber of Gary Owens would use my material on the radio. And one day I get a call to appear in George Schlatter's office. George Schlatter was the producer of *Laugh In*. And this is when *Laugh In* was getting 50 shares.

And I'm like, what does George Schlatter want with me? So, I go to the meeting obviously. And apparently, unbeknownst to me, Gary submitted my comedy material to him. And George Schlatter offered me a job as a writer on *Laugh In*. And it's funny, we laughed about it because George is still around and he was a guest on my podcast, and I talked about this.

And I said, "Can I do this part time or from home?" And he goes, "What? No, this is a job. You come to the office every day. We're paying you a lot of money to write on the number one show in America." And I said I would lose my 2S deferment and I would wind up drafted in Vietnam. So, I couldn't take it. I had to turn down *Laugh In*. So, I was almost a writer six years before I actually broke in.

Okay. So how did you end up then meeting up with David Isaacs?

Ken Levine: Like I said, I became a disc jockey out of college. My draft number was four. And like I said, I was at KMPC and one of our disc jockeys, Roger Carroll, was one of the main AFRTS (The Armed Forces Radio and Television Service) disc jockeys.

I shopped around looking, is there a decent reserve unit I could join that would keep me out of the army? And I saw that there was an armed forces radio reserve unit in LA. And through Roger, he helped pull some strings and got me in the unit. It's like one of those things where you get a call saying, "Okay, there's an opening in the unit, but you got to go down to Torrance and sign up for it tomorrow." And so you don't have time to think, "Boy, do I want to risk this? Is there a way I can get a medical thing?"

And it's six years. It's a six-year commitment. Go. So that's what I did. I got into that unit. And we were at summer camp three years later and somebody new to the unit was David Isaacs. And we met and started talking and we both kind of had desires to be writers.

And when summer camp ended, I was at the time working as a disc jockey in San Bernardino. I got fired, which was a frequent occurrence. And I came back home to live with my parents in LA. And I called David and I said, "Hey, remember me from the army? I want to try writing a script. You want to try writing it with me?"

And he said, "Okay." And so, we got together and decided to partner up and we wrote a pilot. But we didn't know anything. We had no clue what we were doing. And I had to literally go to a bookstore in Hollywood and on a remainder table were TV scripts. And so, for two dollars I bought a copy of an episode of *The Odd Couple* and looked at that.

Oh, "Interior Madison Apartment Day." That's what that is. This is the format, and this is how long they are. So, David and

I wrote a pilot about two kids in college, which was the sum total of our life experience back then. We were both 23. And it didn't go anywhere, obviously. But we had a good time doing it. And we then learned the way to break in is to write spec scripts from existing shows.

So that's what we did. And eventually we broke in.

So, had you written anything with him before that or seen any of his writing? What was it that made you think this is the guy?

Ken Levine: He just seemed like a funny guy. Neither of us had written anything. Neither of us had any writing samples for the other. No, we just sat down together and just tried doing it. It probably was a help that we were both starting from the same place, which was nowhere. It's just kind of one of those happy accidents where you go on a blind date, and it turns out to be your wife.

How many years did you guys write together?

Ken Levine: Well, we're still writing together, if somebody would hire us. Fifty years.

Congratulations.

Ken Levine: October of 1973 is when we started.

And I'm trying to remember, was it *The Tony Randall Show* or *The Jeffersons* where you sold your first script?

Ken Levine: *The Jeffersons.*

And how did that happen?

Ken Levine: Well, we had written a spec *Mary Tyler Moore* and a spec *Rhoda*, and another spec pilot. Which was better but didn't go anywhere.

And one day my mom is playing golf with a guy who says he's the story editor of *The Jeffersons*, a new show that just came on. My mom says, "Oh, well, my son is a great young writer." And he's like, "Oh Christ." And he says, "All right, well, just have him call me."

So, I called him, and the guy says, "You have a script?" And I said, "Yeah." And he goes, "All right, send the script. If I like the script, we'll talk." And I sent off our *Mary Tyler Moore Show*. And I got a letter back saying, "Oh, this is a really good script. Make an appointment, come on in and pitch stories." And we pitched stories, and they bought one. And so that's how we got our assignment.

Thinking back, is there one moment that you felt like was really pivotal that officially launched you guys?

Ken Levine: Yeah, doing that first *MASH.* episode. We had done *The Jeffersons*, we had done episodes of *Joe and Sons*, which was a terrible show on CBS. We had done some stories for *Barney Miller*, but Danny Arnold always cut us off before we got to script. We did a backup script for a pilot that didn't go. And then we got *MASH.* And our first episode of *MASH,* which is the one where the gas heater blows up and Hawkeye is temporarily blind. And that script was like our golden ticket.

It's a very memorable episode.

Ken Levine: Oh, thank you. I remember it.

I spoke with—I don't know if you know her—April Smith. And she said she learned everything she learned about writing in a room from Gene Reynolds. Where did you learn about writing in a room?

Ken Levine: Well, I don't know about writing in a room from Gene, because we never worked in a room, really, with Gene.

But I learned more about storytelling, and more about story construction from Gene Reynolds than everybody else combined. I've been very lucky to have a lot of great mentors along the way, or to work with really talented writers and be smart enough to just shut up and listen and learn from them. But if I had to pick one true mentor, it would be Gene Reynolds. I cannot say enough about Gene Reynolds. I owe my career to Gene Reynolds.

What was his special gift?

Ken Levine: First of all, he was very much a gentleman. So, when he would give you notes, if he didn't like a joke, he wouldn't go, "Jesus, guys, what the fuck?" He would go, "And, um, you might take another look at this. You might take another look at that joke." Okay.

Gene had a great story sense that was combined with a real humanity. It had to be more than just funny. It had to be grounded. There had to be, like I said, humanity to it. And the humanity and nice moments and things had to be earned. And he was very clever in constructing stories where things were set up and then got paid off in a somewhat surprising way. Looking for inventive, different ways of finding a solution. It's why to me, storytelling is always so hard, because each time you tell a story, you want it to be different. You don't want to just keep retelling the same story over and over again.

And Gene would look at a thing and go, "Is there a better way of conveying this? Is there something more interesting that Hawkeye could do once he learns this information?"

You could give Gene an outline. And everyone can go, "Okay, well, this doesn't work." Gene could go, "This doesn't work, and here's why, and here's how you can fix it. If Radar knows this, and then HotLips does this, then you could do a fun thing where it's a thing and..."

And you're going, "Man, he just solved it. Just solved it." I thank him for that.

He was very tough on story, which I took from him. And again, there's the humanity aspect of it, which normally you think, well, okay, that's just part of it. But when I see shows today—and I know I'm going to sound like, you know, an old guy, "get off my lawn"— but when I see shows today, like *White Lotus* and a lot of these other shows that are just mean spirited. Where the laughs are coming from watching horrible people do horrible things to each other.

Look, comedy changes and society changes, et cetera. But to me, there has to be some heart to it. There has to be some, some humanity. And that was so drummed into me by Gene.

Gene also talked about the value of research, which I have learned a lot.

You know, you go off to write a project about whatever. You're going to do a pilot about the Department of Motor Vehicles. You sort of know a lot about the Department of Motor Vehicles. You've stood in the lines and everything. Gene would say, "Go there. Talk to those people. What is that job really like? What do they really do? And immerse yourself in that world." And that's what I've always done since.

Jim Brooks, who worked with Gene on *Room 222*, learned the value of research from Gene. And when Jim Brooks did *Broadcast News*, he spent a tremendous amount of time in newsrooms, talking to those people, getting a sense of authenticity. It requires work. It requires a lot of extra legwork, but it makes the scripts richer and more authentic. And it's worth putting in the time and effort.

I just had Michael Connelly on as a guest on my podcast. And one of the things I asked him—he does the *Bosch* books and *The Lincoln Lawyer* and is my favorite mystery writer—and I said, "So with all the detectives out there, what's so special about yours and your books?"

And he said, "The authenticity." He spent years on the crime beat at *The Los Angeles Times* and really got to know the inside workings of the LAPD. There is an authenticity to his books that you don't get with a lot. It makes a difference.

Research pays off. Okay, one more TV question. What inspired your move into directing?

Ken Levine: I'd been a writer for many, many years. A lot of those years I was on staff of a show. And years when I wasn't on staff on a show—since I'm a good joke guy—I would get a job as a consultant on a show. Meaning, I would work one night a week, which was always rewrite night.

What a great gig.

Ken Levine: It was a great gig. You worked long hours, but it was a great gig. And at the time the pay was ridiculous. There was one season I was on four shows. So, I was working basically four nights till two, three o'clock in the morning. And it got to the point where I would go down to the stage and I would kind of dread going down to the stage, because all I was worried about was, "Okay, let this not be a train wreck. Okay, let this be in good shape, so that I can go home at ten or eleven or twelve."

And I thought to myself, "There's something wrong here. You get into the business, you should want to be on the stage." So, I thought, be a director and be on the stage and play all day with the actors. And then when it comes time for rewriting, "Good luck guys. You go to the room and rewrite, and I'll go to a Laker game."

So that was my motivation. It should be fun. If you're in television and you're in multi-camera shows, you should look forward to going down to the stage. And if you don't, then it's time to change things around. So, that was my motivation.

Did you feel like you had any advantages as a director because of your background in writing and your understanding of scene construction?

Ken Levine: Yes. Number one: The writing served me very well. I was talking to Jim Burrows once, who is the Mozart of TV comedy directors. And I was asking him about shots and this and that. And he said, "Look, if the story works, you can have one camera and just shoot the master of the whole show and it'll work. And if the story doesn't work, you can have all the camera angles and cutting you want. It's not gonna save it."

So yes, it was a big help to me, having that experience, being able to say to the actors, "Okay, I see what's wrong here. You need help with the script. You need a few more lines before you can get this angry. Okay. The reason why you're having trouble here is you have to go from zero to seventy in two lines. And you need help here."

And I was also able—this is something Jimmy did and no other director I know of other than me would do the same thing—and that is, we would go back to the writer's room after the run through and I would sit with the guys while we would discuss what was wrong and what needed to be fixed. And I would kind of help them along that line as much as I could, which proved to be very helpful.

And also, it was very helpful because you go down to the stage the next morning and you have your table reading. And you're able to say to the cast, "Okay, this is what they did last night. These were the problems. This is how they addressed it." And there were certain things where actors would go, "Where's my joke?" And you're able to say, "The script was long. It was not you. You did a good job with the joke. The script was really long. It's a joke that was easily liftable as opposed to something that was more integral to moving the story forward. That's why you lost the joke."

So, it helped in communication. Also, by that time I had been a showrunner. So, I was used to coming down to the stage, and if I saw something I didn't like—with blocking or something—I'd go, "Wait a minute, why is she here and she over there? This is a private conversation. Put them together. Why are they standing back there in the corner? Why did you put them at this table? The audience can't see them over here. You put them over here at this front table, and then we can have background and you can have some depth and geography and stuff like that." So, I have that aspect.

I also spent a lot of time editing these shows. So, I would work with the editor, and I'd say, "Okay, go to the wide shot where we see the full costume." And he goes, "We don't have it." "Wait, what? It's a costume joke. He comes in dressed like Mr. Pickwick and you only have it up to here?" So, as a director, I go, "Okay, this is what I need to make this joke."

And also reaction shots are so important. You know, when the director is directing a multi camera show—which is like directing Rubik's cube—you have a camera coordinator who works with you, making sure that all the shots are right. And so, he'll go down the script and it's like, "Okay, Kelsey's line. All right, we have Kelsey on camera A, and then his line we have on camera C and then Roz we have here." And he's making sure that everything is covered. But I also want reaction shots. They aren't in the script, but I know when Sam says this, you're going to want to cut to Diane's reaction to it. So, I had that going in my head.

And also knowing like, "Okay, this show is running a little long. I suspect that they may cut this section of a scene." So, when I block it and when I set my cameras, do it in such a way where you can make that lift. Don't have somebody cross the stage during that section, because then if you lift it, the guy pops onto the other side of the room. Don't just have a master, so that there's nothing to cut away to.

So, there's like all kinds of things that are going through your head besides just directing the actors that my experience was able to help me with.

Well, you said Rubik's Cube, and that's what it sounds like: a Rubik's Cube on stage.

Ken Levine: You've got five, six people on stage, and you have four cameras. You want to get a master and singles and reaction shots and two shots. And it's all happening fluidly while the scene is going on. And then when somebody moves around the couch, then the cameras have to move, and are you covered? And those guys are amazing, the camera people in LA. If you're nice to them.

I remember there was an episode of *Becker* that I was directing, and it was in the diner. And somebody had to go way upstage in the corner to the coat rack. And so, as I'm camera blocking that scene, I'm saying, "All right, I'm going to have to do a pickup. Fred, I'm going to have to send you way up the line to give me Ted in the corner there."

And he said, "I can get there." And I go, "Fred, you have like a line and a half, you know, because I've got you on Reggie. And then they cut away to Bob saying, 'I looked at my lunch pail and

I didn't have anything.' That's all the time you've got. You've got three seconds to get up there and frame it and do it."

And he says, "I get it. I can get it for you." And for them, that was kind of part of the fun, was sort of the challenge. If they like you. If they don't like you, good luck.

Where did *Must Kill TV*, the novel, come from?

Ken Levine: It came from—originally—an idea that David and I had.

And this is kind of weird: We wrote this as a screenplay, we're talking about it, and we start plotting it out. And I went to sleep at night, and I dreamed the whole book. And I got up three in the morning and I took a pencil and I just wrote down very quickly all of the beats and all of the moves.

And when we came into work, I said to David, "So I had this dream sort of version of the thing. Maybe we can use some of this, maybe this could be sort of a starting point." And David read it and said, "That's the outline."

So, we wrote it as a screenplay that didn't go anywhere. And I always kind of wanted to write a comic novel. My favorite book in the world is *A Confederacy of Dunces*. I read it in the late seventies for the first time.

And so, I sort of had an idea for a comic novel. I started writing it in like 1980-81, when we had a development deal to create pilots and I had more time. At the time, I wrote it longhand and then would type it. And then I would go back. And I'm at, like, a hundred pages. And I'm figuring, "God, this book's going to be 9,000 pages." So, I'd go back and I would cut and stuff and never kind of really got through it. And then we got *Cheers* and I just put it aside. And I never went back to it.

And maybe five, six years ago, I came across the manuscript, 80 pages. And as I'm reading it, it's like, "Where was I going with this?" I have no idea. The outline is long gone. I have no idea where I was going with this. So that was my first attempt.

So, when I decided to write a comic novel, I thought, "Okay, this will be fun." And the thing that I wanted to achieve with the novel is: "If I'm going to write a novel, what can I do that I can't do when I'm writing a script?"

And the answer is, get in the guy's head, what the guy is thinking. That was my main reason for choosing that subject. Because I thought, okay, I want to slowly, we see this guy get progressively crazier and crazier and crazier. And that was a whole rich element that we couldn't do in the screenplay.

The screenplay was basically kind of a bare bones outline of what happened. And I embellished quite a bit from the screenplay. I added new characters and added things along the way. My main goal was getting into the guy's head and see him get progressively crazier and crazier as I continued to tighten the vice.

You did indeed. You get him up in the tree and you just throw rocks at him.

Ken Levine: Oh, yeah. Good comedy writers are sadists. It's like, have a character, take him out of his comfort zone, and watch what happens. See what he can do. And keep the pressure applied.

So that screenplay acted just for you as a pretty solid outline, from which you could veer off?

Ken Levine: Yes. Very little, if any of the dialogue from the screenplay is used in the book. I started from scratch.

And you also had years and years of research of the TV business, just by dint of having been in the TV business.

Ken Levine: Right, right. I did not have experience with having an affair, but my wife would not let me do that research.

Well, you faked it pretty good.

Ken Levine: Yeah.

So, as you were working on the novel, did you find that there were specific tricks that you had learned as a TV writer that you were applying to your novel writing, when it came to exposition or dialogue or pace?

Ken Levine: Yes. Keep the pace going, keep the story moving. What was hard for me is when you write screenplays, television, all of the stage direction is in present tense. I had to go back and now suddenly put things in past tense. And that was a struggle.

And in dialogue, when to break up the rhythm with 'he said' or 'she poured us a cup of coffee,' and all of those interjections? Working those in, because my dialogue has a flow to it, there's like a rhythm to my dialogue. And now I had these interjections and somehow had to keep that flow while making it clear. Because if you don't—I know there are books where it's just dialogue, dialogue, dialogue, dialogue. And you're going, "Wait, who said what?" Like after the third one, you're going, "Wait, which one is this?"

Especially if it's lines like, "I don't know. He didn't tell me." You're going, "Wait, did <u>she</u> say that? Or did <u>he</u> say that?" So, I needed to work that in.

And I got a lot of help from Lee Goldberg, who is a mystery writer and a former TV writer. He was helpful.

Do you remember specifically any suggestions he offered you?

Ken Levine: Yeah. He thought my original beginning was awful.

It's great having friends, isn't it, who can talk to you honestly?

Ken Levine: Well, he was right. I went back and reconceived how to start the book. And I don't even remember how it was I started the book. But he was like, "You've got to suck the reader in. You've got to do that. We need to know certain things quickly."

And he was right. I completely rewrote the beginning and gave it to him. He was like, "Okay, yeah, good. Yeah, much better."

Beth Ciotta, she writes romance novels, but she was very helpful. I didn't know about head hopping originally. So, she read an early draft and said, "Well, you got head hopping going on here." "What's that?"

It's not a problem in TV writing.

Ken Levine: Yeah, it's like how a person's mind is working. And what his thought process is. It's got to be one at a time—you can go to a new chapter and a different character or a new section. But you can't have "Fred sat there wondering what she meant by that," and then go to her and "She's wondering what Fred thought." You can't do that. I didn't know that. Okay, so I had to go back and change that. They're rookie mistakes.

Well, it's just not something you were used to doing. How was the process of being alone in a room writing? Because for fifty years you've been in the room with somebody else writing. What was that like?

Ken Levine: There's parts of it I really like and parts of it that I don't.

The part I like is that I can do whatever I want to do without having to sell it to somebody else. Without having to explain it. And if I want to go off on a tangent and try something and write three pages and then go, "Nah, this doesn't work," I can just throw it out.

But I do miss the social aspect of it. Because you're right: you sit here all day. And I go out and get lunch and I'm sitting there reading a book. And my wife comes home and it's like, I haven't spoken to a soul until six o'clock at night. And it's nice to have that social interaction and someone to get lunch with. And someone to do half the work with. And especially with a comedy, somebody who can make you laugh or whose opinion you value. So, if he says, "Nah, I think we can do better." So, there was that aspect of it.

Early on in our career, we would once a year—we always wrote head-to-head, we always wrote where we're both in the same room. We would dictate our scripts. We would have a secretary take shorthand, and we would dictate the script to the secretary. Once a year, we would take a script and split it up, and I would write half, and he would write half. And then we would put the two together, and we would do the rewrite together.

And first of all, it was hard to tell who wrote which act. But we did this so that we felt comfortable writing on our own, so we were a partnership out of choice and not dependent. It's not like, "Yeah, I know I'm an hour late every day, but I'm the funny one." We always knew we could write separately. We chose to write together. We just felt that the sum total of the work between us would be better than the solo efforts.

When it came to rewriting, did you do a humor pass just to go through and add or polish jokes. Or was that going on the whole time?

Ken Levine: It was going on the whole time. We never did vomit drafts.

There are some writers that will just do vomit drafts, just so that they have something on paper and then they go back. We never did that. Like I said, we would dictate the script to the secretary. She would give me the pages at the end of the day, and I would proofread it. And then when we were finished with the draft, we would each get a copy, and we would each make notes. And then we went and did a second draft together.

There were two things that we would always try to do with the second draft. First is, add five really good jokes. Somewhere add five really good jokes. And number two is, if there was a long speech, cut it down. There were always ways of trimming long speeches. You could always find a way to cut it down.

And more often than not, we would be rewriting, and I would say, "I think we can beat this joke." And it was my joke. So, we were very tough on jokes. "Yeah, it's funny. Maybe there's something funnier. Let's see, is there a different way of going here?" So that's what we would usually do with the second draft. And then that was usually it.

Back to the novel. We talked earlier about pace—the book has a constant moving forward pace to it. But you also, very cleverly end each chapter with something that required me to keep reading. Whether it was a joke that led to something or it was a foreshadowing of something. Do you think you learned to do that as well as you did in the book because of act breaks on TV?

Ken Levine: Absolutely. Absolutely. And it goes beyond the act break, it's the way we would end scenes. We would do that in scenes just to keep you going. Anything you can to hook the reader. I mean, it's storytelling. It's just, how do you hold on to a reader and keep him?

Does that take us back to Gene Reynolds?

Ken Levine: Yes. You look at those *MASH* episodes and we had two, sometimes three stories going at the same time, and dovetailing, and cleverly coming together.

Really, really artful. Okay, one last question. For any aspiring novelists who are reading or listening, is there one piece of advice that you'd give them based on your experience as a screenwriter and a TV writer?

Ken Levine: Don't bore me, okay? Don't bore me. When you spend four pages describing the hotel room, you're boring me. When you spend three pages discussing how you make a sauce, you're boring me.

Don't bore me.

MATT GOLDMAN

Matt Goldman is a highly accomplished writer who has found success in both the television and literary worlds. He got his start writing for the iconic sitcom Seinfeld in the early 90s. Goldman went on to write for numerous other hit TV comedies like Ellen, The New Adventures of Old Christine, and the cult sci-fi series Dirk Gently's Holistic Detective Agency, amassing over 500 episodic writing credits.

More recently, Goldman pivoted to novel writing and has made his mark in the crime fiction genre. His debut novel Gone to Dust introduced readers to private investigator Nils Shapiro and the Twin Cities setting Goldman knows so well. The Nils Shapiro series, which now spans four books, has earned Goldman prestigious nominations like the Shamus and Nero Awards.

One key takeaway from the interview is Goldman's emphasis on always keeping the story entertaining, no matter the medium. As he advises aspiring novelists (and echoes our last interviewee, Ken Levine): "If you want to do it for a living, don't be boring."

So, let's start from the beginning, because I'm really curious about this. I'm Minneapolis born and raised. And I know you started out here doing standup. Was that at the old Mickey Finn's? Was it that early? Or did you start later?

Matt Goldman: No, a little later. It was 1983, and it was at Scott Hanson's Comedy Gallery.

So, I probably saw you at some point.

Matt Goldman: Yeah, probably. I was never a headliner back then. Actually, I never became a headliner at all. I jumped ship before reaching that point. But I did work a lot as an opener and middle act.

It was a golden age at that point. There were a lot of places to perform. So, you say you started in stand-up. How did you get into TV writing?

Matt Goldman: I wanted to write television. Soon into my standup career, I realized I enjoyed the writing part more than the performing part. I was often asked to open for national acts when they came through, because my act was clean, not because I was a prude. I just wanted to be on *The Tonight Show,* and I didn't want to waste my time developing anything I couldn't do on *The Tonight Show.* So, I was seen as an ideal opening act.

That's how I met Jerry Seinfeld, opening for him. And Dana Carvey, and Bob Saget, and Dennis Miller, and Roseanne Barr, and a whole bunch of people.

And they all said the same thing: you should write TV. You should write TV. And that's what I wanted to do. And so, I had just turned 24 years old. I got in my dented-up Ford Escort and drove west. And it worked out.

It sure did. What was your first writing assignment?

Matt Goldman: Well, I had some very little writing jobs. It was actually Louie Anderson's agent who took me in as what they call a pocket client. He didn't sign me to the big agency contract, but he kept his ears open for me.

And there were little jobs, punching up game show material, writing some sketches for a kid's show. I punched up some material for what was basically a beauty contest shot in Japan. Little weird jobs like that.

But I had opened for Jerry Seinfeld in Minneapolis, doing ten shows in one week at the Comedy Gallery. We remained friends. We played softball together. He and Joel Hodgson wrote an HBO special for Jerry. Neither of them could type though, and I could type really well. So, I was the typist while those two did it. And I got to pitch some jokes.

And in the meanwhile, I had written a play with a fellow comedian also from the Midwest, named Pat Hazel. And Jerry really liked that play, which debuted at the Comedy Cabaret in 1987 when I was a wee lad.

And when Jerry got his show, he asked me to work on it. I was in the right place at the right time.

With the right skills.

Matt Goldman: Yeah, I had worked hard to learn how to write TV. I used to tape—this is pre internet—I used to videotape sitcoms and then watch them back over and over, trying to graph the storylines, trying to deconstruct how they were written.

And did that help?

Matt Goldman: It did help. It did help quite a bit.

I started to see things I had never thought about before, even though we all know them subconsciously. Like, there was a main story, and then there is a B story, and sometimes a C story. And I could see how they would thread those together, which was very good training for *Seinfeld*. Because what *Seinfeld* started to do was make equal weighted stories that would then all dovetail together at the end in an unexpected way (which was Larry David's genius). But I conceptually could understand what he was doing from my self-education on sitcom stories.

So, when it came to the play, was it *Bunkhouse Buddies*?

Matt Goldman: *Bunkbed Brothers*.

And it was the two of you—Pat Hazell and you—in that cast originally.

Matt Goldman: Yes, it was.

And is that the show where you would order a pizza during the show?

Matt Goldman: Yes, we ordered a pizza during the show, and a real Domino's pizza person would show up. And we would hand them a script to do their lines.

That's fantastic. And Pat Hazell said one of the reasons you did it was because you weren't making any money, and it was a way to get fed.

Matt Goldman: Yeah. Boy, that first time we did that show, it was by the seat of our pants. But that's what you do in your twenties. It was fun.

And that became a great writing sample for you, as I remember from what Pat said.

Matt Goldman: Yes, that's what got me *Seinfeld* in many ways. And Pat came on too. He wrote a lot of the interstitial stand-up material for Jerry that was between scenes in the earlier seasons. And we got a movie deal out of that play. We got a TV deal out of that play. We got a lot of mileage out of it.

And did that grow into the pilot and several episodes about the two brothers working in the lawn and garden store?

Matt Goldman: Yes. *The Archers of Omaha.* That is what that was. And NBC at the last minute decided not to air it because it was the only comedy they had that wasn't set in New York. And they thought it would be confusing to the audience to have this Midwestern show that takes place in a lawn and garden center. And it's too bad, because we really had a lot of fun making that show and I'm proud of it.

I don't know if I read you having said this, or Pat saying it, but the network objected to the use of the word "corn."

Matt Goldman: Yeah. There were a lot of things they didn't want us to say. Like "corn," which is crazy. It was crazy.

But Pat said that was a great tool because, he'd say, "Throw in the word 'corn,' and that's what they'd focus on." And you could get away with other stuff.

Matt Goldman: Yes, that is true. That is a thing that served me very well over the years as a television writer, putting in things we knew the network would flag. And then they felt like they did their job, and they would leave the rest of the script alone.

So, was there a point after *Seinfeld* that you felt was sort of pivotal, where things sort of clicked and you went, "Now I'm in the groove"?

Matt Goldman: Yeah, and it was after *Seinfeld*. Because I was there in the very beginning of *Seinfeld*, and I learned so much from Larry and Jerry by their example. Mostly about standing up for your vision, sticking to your voice, sink or swim on your own merits. Don't take notes from the network that will sink you and then let them blame you for the show's demise.

But I didn't really learn how to write *Seinfeld,* because Larry and Jerry were just so busy writing it themselves. It was not a traditional writer's room. There were just a few of us there. And maybe because I didn't grow up with them or grow up in New York, I mean, I contributed, but I didn't really grasp what that show was about until a few years after I was off it. And I realized, "Oh, this isn't a show about nothing. This is a show about selfishness." That's what that show is. And had I understood that then, I think I would have stayed. Because I asked to leave because I could tell I wasn't getting it.

And then I went on and worked for more traditional shows and traditional showrunners. And I started to really understand. "Oh, this is how you make a TV show." I mean, *Seinfeld* being my first show, that was both the greatest and the worst thing that could have happened to me. Overall, the greatest because —even though that's not my voice and that's not what I write in my books—what I learned about standing up for your voice and vision is what allows me to write my books.

But I didn't really learn. I didn't learn about casting very much or editing or those other things writers do until the next show I worked on.

And what show was that, and why was that different? Was it more traditional?

Matt Goldman: Yes, and it was very well run. It was a show that some people remember and some people don't. It was called *Love and War.* It was on CBS.

It was created by Diane English, who had created *Murphy Brown.* Diane's a very good writer and a very good showrunner. I was thirty years old, and I was with all these writers who were in their mid-forties. And they were so good to me and took me under their wing. And then I started getting taken to casting and editing and set design meetings and set decorating meetings and looking at the props and all these things TV writers do. They're the producers.

That show was not as good of a show as *Seinfeld* in any way, shape or form. But I did learn a lot more about the nuts and bolts of how to produce a television show.

Am I wrong in remembering this about Diane English? Up until then, sitcoms had been Act 1 and Act 2, with a commercial break in between. And she was the one who said, "I can't work that way, I need a three-act structure. So, we're going to have Act 1, a commercial break, Act 2, a commercial break, and then Act 3."

Matt Goldman: I don't know if it was Diane who did that. I honestly can't remember. When I started, everything was two acts. And then, I don't remember when it happened, it moved to three acts. And then, at one point, some shows went to four acts, which was just more commercials. Because when I started, a half hour tv show was actually 22 or 23 minutes long. And the rest of it was commercials. And then it kept getting shorter and shorter over the years.

It got down to like under 20 minutes.

From a 'breaking a story' standpoint, did you find it easier to work in 2 acts or 3 acts, or did it not make a difference?

Matt Goldman: I don't think it makes a difference. I'm not a big believer in all that structure stuff. And I think that if structure is your main concern, you're more likely to write something formulaic, because you're trying to hit those beats by a certain time.

And then a show comes along and breaks the rules. I had friends who worked on *Everybody Loves Raymond*. I didn't. But sometimes they would do two scenes, two acts. One long scene, one more long scene. That was the end of the show.

Which is actually a throwback to *I Love Lucy*. *I Love Lucy* did that all the time.

Matt Goldman: You know, those shows that feel more like plays are what I tend to love.

So on like *Friends*, which might have six scenes in an act—

Matt Goldman: —Yes, I think *Seinfeld* started that, those very short scenes. More story, more movement, more characters having stories, not just a character having a story and other characters supporting them. But *Seinfeld* was really on the front end of that.

And that makes for a much longer shoot night.

Matt Goldman: Yes, it does. It does.

You sort of touched on this, but is there one point in this process where the idea of how to best tell a story really clicked? Is there a moment when you went, "Oh, I get it. That's how it's done." Or was it just an osmosis over several series?

Matt Goldman: I think it was an evolution. Story was the hardest thing to learn for me. I think character came to me naturally. Dialogue came to me naturally. Joke writing came to me naturally, because of stand-up. Story was hard for me to learn, but eventually I figured it out.

Is there any secret to it?

Matt Goldman: Yeah, it's not really a secret. Other people know this.

Start it as late as you can, so things are already in motion.

Have characters who want things, but want different things from each other, so they're in conflict.

And don't be boring. Keep it moving. That's the main thing.

What inspired the move from TV writing after doing—as we've tried to add up—over 500 episodes, having your hand in those? What made you decide this is the time to start writing novels? Was that something you'd always wanted to do?

Matt Goldman: I had always wanted to do it from the very beginning. I didn't really have the confidence. I had put that medium on a pedestal. I had always been a big reader since I was a kid. It happens to be my favorite medium, not because it's better, it's just the one I find to be the most intimate relationship with the creative force behind the book.

And I am an introvert. I'm an introvert with social skills. I'm totally fine out in the world. And I can carry my own in a writer's room, but I find it exhausting. But I'd always wanted to try working by myself.

But, you know, in TV they keep you very busy. They pay you well. I had kids.

But I had a break in 2015. I was splitting my time between Minneapolis and Los Angeles and had a break of four months between two TV shows. I knew I was going to go to work in four months. I had been thinking I was going to switch from comedy to drama, just because I was liking where drama was more than comedy.

And I'd been reading a lot of crime fiction. I'd never read crime fiction really. But I'd been reading a lot to try to prepare myself for drama, what I thought would be police procedurals, things like that. And I kind of fell in love with crime fiction, which I didn't expect to do. And then I had this four-month break, and it was the middle of winter here and it was cold out. And I just sat down and started writing my first book. And it changed my life. And I'm much happier in the book world.

Do you have any novel writing heroes?

Matt Goldman: Well, I had heroes in just the regular book world, like Kurt Vonnegut and Mark Twain. They were my heroes because they wrote in very plain language. I found them very accessible and I loved that.

But it wasn't until I read Raymond Chandler. He was the reason for making me want to try. Because Philip Marlowe narrated the books with a really wry sense of humor, a lot of social observation, but in a drama, a dark story. There was a comedic voice telling a darker story.

And then, after reading Chandler, I thought, 'Oh, I think I know how I can do this.' Not use Chandler's voice. And I'm not comparing myself to Chandler. I'm not in that realm. But I have developed this comedic voice over 30 years. And I can use it to have Nils Shapiro narrate a crime story. And that's what I did. And I just sat down and started writing. And it worked out.

So, the first book, *Gone to Dust*—as a writer myself and as a reader—as I was reading through it, I was so annoyed because you as a first-time crime writer had come up with a crime that is not just a murder. It's a murder, but the way that the criminal has hidden the clues, I don't think has ever been done before. And even though it's a book, it was so visual as to what they were walking into and what they had to deal with.

And if you've watched enough TV crime dramas—we watch a lot of British ones here—there's always the point where the

forensics guy walks in and says, "This scene is tarnished." And it's like, "Well, sorry, buddy, the whole house is tarnished." How did that come to you?

Matt Goldman: Just so people know what you're talking about, the book starts when a person is found murdered in their home. And the body—and in fact, most of the house—is covered in the dust and dirt from hundreds of vacuum cleaner bags. So, there's vacuum cleaner dust everywhere.

It came to me—I say jokingly, but it's not really a joke—that I hate the show *CSI*. So, for fun, I used to try to come up with crimes that they could never solve. And that was one of them.

But I also am a big believer in character is more important than story. There's a big relation between the two, but character is really the most important thing. And so, I wanted a crime that couldn't be solved in the lab.

Until last month, this past month, there had not been any murders in Edina for a very long time. And so there was an inexperienced police department. I set it there, so they'd have to hire a consultant. And I created a crime that couldn't be solved in the lab, so that my protagonist, Nils, would have to really draw from his own life experience to gain insight into the investigation. And by drawing from his own life experience, we get to know Nils.

And that's really what I wanted to do. That was my main objective.

Well, mission accomplished. Absolutely.

Matt Goldman: Thank you.

Are you writing from an outline in that case?

Matt Goldman: Never. We don't have enough time to go into why I don't outline. I mean, for me, I'm a strong believer in not outlining. And that's coming from someone who had to outline over 500 episodes of television.

I think it can often be an outside-in way of approaching a story, which leads to characters not behaving true to themselves. And when you do it inside-out, without an outline—in my experience, you get stuck once in a while, but you work through it. And at the end of your first draft, that's your outline.

But it all happens with your characters up on their feet and moving around and talking. And so, I think it's easier to write something that doesn't have characters acting inconsistently, which makes readers go, "Wait, why, what?" And whenever a character says, "I can't believe I'm going to say this, but..." I know it's because they've been hammered into place to fit a story point that was predetermined.

Right. As opposed to dynamic characters on their feet, dealing with stuff that you're throwing in front of them.

Matt Goldman: Yes. And just being open to change and shifting directions. Now I don't think I could have done that had I not worked on all those episodes of television. Because I've developed a pretty strong sense of when I'm going astray. And then I just have to back up a little bit and find the right path. But I wouldn't have had that story sense had I not had all those late-night hours in a TV writer's room.

Well, your muscle memory is very strong when it comes to what's going to work in a story.

Matt Goldman: Yes.

So, can you think of any specific writing technique that you

used when writing for TV that you have incorporated into your novel writing process?

Matt Goldman: I don't know if it's a technique as much as just the attitude that it's a butt in the chair job. There are no short-cuts. You just have to put in the time. And if you have a bad day, not to let it frustrate you. Just know, "oh, that was a bad day, there'll be a better one tomorrow." And that's really it, as simple as that sounds.

There's a lot I learned from TV that I use in novel writing. I mean, character development, relationship arcs, series architecture. Dialogue is a huge one. Pacing. But not prose. There is no prose writing skills in TV. That I learned from reading.

So, when you started the first one, did you plan that this was going to be a series with Nils Shapiro?

Matt Goldman: I hoped. I mean, I dared to hope, I guess. And when Forge, which is an imprint of Macmillan, made the offer, they said, "We think this is a series." So, when they bought the first one, they ordered a second. And when they read the second, they ordered two more. And I enjoyed it very much, writing that series.

So, with your background in working on TV series and multiple episodes, how did that inform setting up the first book in the series?

Matt Goldman: Well, people do it different ways, but I wanted to have a protagonist who kept growing through the process. And so, I backed him up into a pretty emotionally wounded place. I didn't want to do the cliché of 'he's a hard drinker.' I didn't want to go that route.

But I put him in a place where he's still not over his ex-wife.

And he's dealing with that. And that gave him specific insight into the dust crime, which is why I gave him that situation.

But I really learned that you have to throw a certain number of balls in the air if you want to keep a series going. And create characters who can go from being minor characters up to major characters. And intertwine their relationships.

And all of that I learned from television.

You mentioned character development was something you learned. How did that process help when you're writing a series?

Matt Goldman: Well, the big part of it is you learn that characters really have to have three dimensions to them. They have to have backstories. I'm not somebody who goes and writes their whole backstory out. But they have to have this existing life they bring to the table and things they want, obstacles they've faced in the past. What are their fears? What are their hopes? What are their wounds?

And when you bring characters into a story that have all those dimensions, it just creates a lot of possibility for future stories. Whatever happens in the current story, whatever they experienced from solving that crime will make them a different person, a more knowledgeable person, or maybe even a more wounded person in the next book. So that they're always kind of in motion, which is what we are. We're all in motion.

When people say, "Oh, I'm not myself today," I always say, "Yes, you are. This is how you are today, but you're still yourself." Because we're not snapshots, we're moving. We're moving pictures all the time.

When you were writing the first one—I'm thinking of it sort of like a pilot. You're writing a pilot for the series. And I'm

sure you've read pilots that landed immediately. You read it and went, "Yes, they absolutely know what they're doing." And you've read other pilots where you thought, "They have no idea what's happening in episode two. They have no idea."

Did you find as you were writing the first one—with that pilot mentality in mind—were you laying little Easter eggs for things you thought, "I might not pay this off for four books, but I want to remember this about Nils." Or, "I want to remember this about something that'll turn up later."

Matt Goldman: Yeah, I don't know if I laid Easter eggs as much as I saw situations that could become something.

For instance, Nil's best friend, who's an Edina cop in the first book, they have a history together. I thought, once I wrote that first book, which kind of reunited them, I want this relationship to continue. That character's name is Alagard. He had three kids. I thought, "Oh, I want those kids to, as they grow, to complicate Alagard's life. And maybe Nils can be like an uncle figure and help them." I saw possibilities.

Then in the second book, they hired a junior detective, and I thought that person could play a big role in Nils life. They also reunited with an old friend, they all went to the Minneapolis police Academy together. One of their old cadet friends came back into their life. I thought that could be significant for Nils.

So, I just kind of can see where it can go, but I don't know yet where it's going to go. I just see the possibilities.

But it's good to be thinking like that early on. And that's something you learned, I think, in TV writing.

Matt Goldman: Yeah, it is. And then it makes the characters feel more real to you, because you can see where they've been.

You can see where they might go and that, oh, they're not going to be defined by this one story in one book. They have a bigger life outside of that.

You mentioned dialogue. How did all the TV writing help you figure out what's good dialogue and what's not good dialogue?

Matt Goldman: I think when I became a TV writer, I became a much better listener in real life. I mean, I would not only listen to people say things, even if it's just I was in a coffee shop and I was eavesdropping on a table next to me. I would listen to what they were saying. I would imagine it typed out with the punctuation. The way people really talk, not always in full sentences, stopping, starting, shifting in the middle of the sentence to another idea.

You know, dialogue gets really clunky when writers get lazy about exposition, and they try to fit it into dialogue. And no one ever talks like that. No one ever says, "As you know..." "As we've discussed before." So, I think I really made a concentrated effort to listen to people in real life so that I would not write embarrassing dialogue in scripts. And it helped out quite a bit.

Did you learn any tricks on how to get exposition buried in?

Matt Goldman: I don't know if it's a trick, but boy, try to make it as entertaining as you can. You know, in my fifth book, *Carolina Moonset,* which is not a Nils book, two characters who are in their forties kind of get tricked into going on a first date by their mothers. They're on vacation. And one of them says, "This is a stupid idea. Let's just tell each other all the bad stuff about each other right now. And then if we want to hang out the rest of the week, we can."

And so there is this device where they're just telling each other all the terrible things about themselves, rather than putting on their best first impression.

And so we learned about those characters, but it was in an entertaining way, because they were just bombarding each other with self-deprecating information.

That's a clever way of doing that. You mentioned about structuring stories, the idea of coming in as late as possible, leaving as early as possible. And you've certainly obviously carried that over into the novels, because they zip right along. Did you find that in TV writing where you had to write a cliffhanger scene to get people to come back through the commercial?

Matt Goldman: Absolutely I learned that in TV writing. It's called an act break. And the whole idea was to bring people back after a commercial. When I started, it was all network TV, it was all commercials, there was no streaming. So, you really did want the story to hang at the end of the act, so people would want to see what was going to happen next. And we spent a lot of time as TV writers on those act breaks. And it really helped me in my novel writing.

That's a skill. You're lucky that you had all that experience.

Matt Goldman: No, I am. Very lucky.

What about plot twists? You mentioned the TV shows were pretty well structured by the time you sat down to write them, that you were working from outlines. How do you surprise readers and yourself when you're not working from an outline?

Matt Goldman: I don't know. I mean, I guess it's very important to me that the story keep moving. But it can get boring if it just keeps moving in one direction.

Once I get going, I start to see where it can go. And the further I go, the more I know where it's going. But I also can see in the future: "Oh, it would be great if this happened. Or that happened." And so, then I can kind of build toward that twist.

And, you know, you're selectively revealing information when you're an author. Otherwise, you would just go right to the end.

But I just kind of get a feel for it and see it. And the more I get to know the characters and their dynamics and how they represent themselves to each other, the more possibilities I see for twists.

I am not a fan, even though they're popular, I am not a fan of unreliable narrators. I find the storytelling to be not fair, at least in all the books I've read that have them. So, I don't go that route. But I do always look for the potentials for twists.

I've found that it's so much easier to hide clues and red herrings in novels. As my wife and I are watching a TV show, and the character will just say, "My phone's not working, can I borrow yours." And I'm like, oh boy, okay. That doesn't just happen.

Matt Goldman: Yes, there's a reason that's in there. And it is also very similar to your introduction into show business—magic—in that you are creating a perception, you are diverting the audience's attention at times. And you are using their expectations to bring them one way when you're going to go another way. I know a little bit about magic, I can't do any of it. But being friends with a few really good magicians and spending time with them, I do know a lot of the principles behind it.

And it's the same principles in mystery writing.

Matt Goldman: Yes, very much.

It's time misdirection, it's spatial misdirection. Burying something in a group of three is the best way to hide a clue. Putting it next to a joke is a huge way of doing it. You can get away with murder if you put it next to a joke. Because they just don't know. And then they go back, and it was like you said, it's entirely fair. And I insist that it be entirely fair.

Matt Goldman: And I think they should all be that way.

I mean, when I read mysteries, I don't really care who did it. I just don't. I just want to be along for the ride. And then it's fun to be pleasantly surprised along the way. But if the reader is not there for the characters and their relationships, then it doesn't matter who did it.

Yes, exactly. A couple last things. One is—and this is totally selfish—but I enjoyed so much that the Shapiro books take place, not only in the Twin Cities, but in some cases blocks from my home. I mean, the creek that he walks through in *Gone To Dust*, I played there when I was a kid. Do you find it easier when you're making it up that you already know the locations you're talking about?

Matt Goldman: Yes. And in all my books, even ones set in other places, I know the locations. I do find it easier, because I think that you feel the lifeblood of the place. And I've gone to visit places that I put in books, places that I haven't spent a lot of time in. But I still always try to visit in person.

Because when you know the culture of a place, it really helps inform the story. Because these stories don't happen in vacuums. The culture in the Twin Cities is very different than the culture of Los Angeles, or the culture of the deep South. And so that really helps inform the story.

And it may not be obvious, but it's kind of in the DNA of it, I think.

Matt Goldman: Yeah, it absolutely is. It's in their history. It's in why do people live in that town? If they weren't born there, what are they going there for? What's important to them? Is it to prosper, but do so without sticking out? Is it to make a big, bright name for yourself? Is it to gain power? All those things come into play.

Your use of the suburb of Edina—which is virtually a character in the last book, very much a character and very accurate to the Edina we know—for someone who doesn't live around here, they'll get a really strong sense of that community. Particularly with the Shapiro books, when he crosses France Avenue and he's in Edina as opposed to when he's in Minneapolis, his world is different.

Matt Goldman: Yeah, especially in the winter.

And that really comes across. Finally, one last question for you. For aspiring novelists, do you have one piece of advice that you'd give them based on your past experiences writing for TV?

Matt Goldman: Well, I would say that if you want to make a living as a novelist, know that part of your job is to entertain. That you can have all the social issues you want in there and character examinations and things that are important to you as a person that you want to share on the page.

But if you want to do it for a living, don't be boring.

PHOEF SUTTON

Phoef Sutton is a highly accomplished writer who has found major success across television, films, and novels. His career began as an award-winning playwright before transitioning to TV writing on the iconic sitcom <u>Cheers</u>. Over eight seasons, Sutton worked his way up to executive producer, winning two Emmys.

This proved invaluable training for Sutton's subsequent work writing for acclaimed shows like <u>NewsRadio</u>, <u>Boston Legal</u>, <u>Terriers</u>, and <u>Chesapeake Shores</u>. While continuing his prolific TV career, Sutton also became a published novelist, drawing from his screenwriting talents to craft compelling novels like the <u>Crush</u> series.

Sutton has also collaborated on book series with notable authors. He contributed to Lee Goldberg's Dead Man series, which brought together various writers to pen linked novels around a central character. Sutton has also partnered with bestselling author Janet Evanovich on her popular novel series.

A key piece of advice Sutton offers writers is the importance of purposeful scene-writing that propels the story forward. As he puts it: *"Every scene has to fulfill a purpose in telling the story. There has to be a reason for every scene to be there."*

I understand that you wrote and acted in plays in high school and in college. Was that always the goal to be a writer or was acting a goal?

Phoef Sutton: Well, yeah, acting was a goal. When I came out here, I sort of thought I wanted to be a writer or an actor. And I decided I could only take getting rejected in one field at a time.

And I thought getting rejected as a writer was more pleasant, because they don't do it to your face. I just didn't get any traction as an actor. I'm really glad that I did it when I did it, because it's very helpful for a screenwriter or television writer to have acted—to have known what it's like to be on the stage and to have to say the words. I can communicate with actors, I think, a little bit better than a lot of other showrunners who've just been writers. Because I know what it's like. I can understand that.

And also, I think I learned—maybe from being an actor or being around actors—I learned how to write for particular people. I mean, when I know a person and I know their voice and I know what they feel. I could write for Treat Williams. I could write for Bob Newhart. I could write for Brian Dennehy. They have different cadences, different ways of speaking. Ted Danson, Kelsey Grammer, Woody Harrelson. And I was able to do that. So that stood me in good stead.

And also, being a playwright, I mean, there aren't very many writers who start as playwrights nowadays. I think, just because there isn't really much theater in this country, or at least not in this city anyway. And I was in plays I wrote, too, so, I mean, there you have nobody to blame but yourself. You can't say, "Who wrote this shit," or, "That actor screwed it up."

And the first thing that I did professionally—aside from some plays in regional theaters, where I got paid a stipend—was *Cheers*. And that was basically a play: the entrances, exits, one set, all that. And all the actors were theater actors. It was a play.

They do stage plays of various sitcoms over the years. They've done *The Golden Girls* and all that. And I'm surprised they haven't done one of *Cheers*, because it's a play.

And that set, that beautiful set, which was designed by Richard Sylbert, who did *Chinatown* and all sorts of other movies. *Who's Afraid of Virginia Woolf.* It was a beautiful set. It was a beautiful set. So many episodes of *Cheers* were just on the set. I mean, we're just on the bar, never left the bar. Never even changed days, because we found that when we filmed in front of an audience on Tuesday nights—and we filmed pretty much the whole thing in front of an audience—we found that (this was later on in the run), we found that when we would have them change their costumes to be a day later, you could never get them (the actors) back. They would go to the dressing rooms, they would start playing foosball, smoking pot, and you could never get them back.

So, there are plenty of episodes of *Cheers* that take place in one day that couldn't possibly have taken place in one day. But we just figured, we don't want to do the costume changes.

I remember hearing an interview with (director) Jim Burrows where he talked about Norm's entrance in the pilot. And he said he felt bad for the writers, because in the blocking, he put Norm at the far end of the bar. Which meant every time Norm came in, you guys needed to write a joke to get him across the room.

Phoef Sutton: Well, it was one of the trademarks of the show. And so, it was good in that sense. But yes, and everyone had to top the one before. At first, there were very simple jokes. But then they had to be, you know, very complex jokes or philosophical jokes.

We would go to great lengths not to have Norm enter; we would have Norm there at the beginning of the show. We didn't want to deal with it.

I wanted to do an episode where they put in a new parking meter in front of the place. So, he had to constantly go and feed the meter. So, there would be like ten Norm entrances in it. And people wanted to kill me for doing that.

Let's just back up real quick here. I want to talk about your playwriting, because I know you had sort of a learning experience, you got an understanding of how the business works with your play *Burial Customs*. About how things look like they're going to happen. And then they don't happen.

Phoef Sutton: I was just out of graduate school at the University of Florida, and I moved to New York for a brief period of time. I couldn't really get in, couldn't get an apartment, couldn't get a job. But there was a brief period of time when Ulu Grossbard, who was a big director, wanted to direct that play. And it was very exciting.

If I'd known more about the business, I would have been more excited *[LAUGHS]* because he just done *Crimes of the Heart* on Broadway. And he was really, really big and he was really into the play. I went to his office on—I don't know, on Times Square or something like that, I don't know where it was—but I felt like I was a part of the Broadway scene.

And then he just sort of lost interest and it went away.

And that sort of thing happens over and over and over again with people in the business. Even if you're very successful, there are millions of times when things look like they're going to be great and then they fall apart.

And my initial reaction to that was to say, "I'm not going to get excited about anything until it's real. Until it's really happening." So that if I sold a script, a pilot script, I wouldn't get excited until they agreed to make the pilot. And then when they did the pilot, I wouldn't get excited until it was on the air. And then when it was on the air, I wouldn't get excited until it lasted. And then I realized that I was putting myself in a position where I never got excited about anything.

So, then I changed my attitude to get excited about every little victory of what comes on. I was right to be excited about Ulu Grossbard doing the play. It was a wonderful opportunity. It didn't pan out. There was nothing wrong with being excited.

You know, you aren't punished for being excited about something that doesn't come to the ultimate conclusion. I mean, even when we won our Emmys for *Cheers*, I basically wouldn't be excited, because I would think, "Well, I've got to go back there tomorrow and do it again."

So now I allow myself to be excited about things.

That's a very good lesson to learn. To find that balance.

Phoef Sutton: It's a hard lesson to learn.

So, what happened with playwriting that got you into TV writing? What was that connection?

Phoef Sutton: I wanted to write for movies. I wanted to write for movies and I wanted to write for television. I wanted to write for theater and I wanted to write books. I wanted to be a writer. I wanted to be a writer, in one form or another.

So, as I said, I couldn't get into New York. I couldn't get a job, couldn't get an apartment. And in LA, I had a relative that I could stay with. And my brother was with the Crown Books chain. So, I knew I could get a clerk job at a Crown Bookstore. I knew I could get a job.

So, I moved to LA with my then fiancé. And I just wrote plays, wrote screenplays. I had a friend from college, Barbara Hall, who was on *Newhart* at the time. She's since gone on to do everything. She did *Madam Secretary* and *I'll Fly Away* and all that.

And so I wrote a spec *Newhart* (script), because she was on *Newhart*. And that was what got me the freelance *Cheers* job.

I didn't know anything about writing for television. I didn't know anything about writing with a group, writing with a room. I was a very private writer, wrote by myself, didn't talk to anybody about what I was writing until it was done. So, I had to learn all that stuff.

I had to learn how to pitch. I had to learn how to pitch in the room during the rewrites. It was really my graduate school, *Cheers*. And it was a good graduate school, because obviously there were the best writers in the business on that show.

So, you're learning from some really, really good people.

Phoef Sutton: Absolutely. Absolutely. Absolutely. And it was very tense. It was very stressful. It was a hard room.

Why was it hard?

Phoef Sutton: Well, because you had to be funny. You had to be good. You had to say the right thing. You had to do it. I mean, there were long silences in the room, where people were thinking and crafting and doing stuff, and trying to do it.

I didn't speak for the first six months in the room, I think. And I think that was probably a good choice. Because the year I joined the staff, two other writers joined the staff too. And I was the only one who made it all the way through the year. They were both let go. And I think part of the reason was that I knew my place. *[LAUGHS]*

I didn't talk first. And then I would try a few jokes and they got laughs. I would try a few more jokes and they would get laughs. And then before you know it, you're doing it and you're just in the zone. It's a difficult thing to describe.

Were you breaking stories as a group?

Phoef Sutton: Yeah. Oh yeah. Every story on that show was broken as a group. We never came in with a story.

At the beginning of each season, Glen and Les (Charles) would come in and we would talk about what to do. And it was very clear that they hadn't thought about it for an instant over the break. And everything was, you know, what do we do? What do we do? What do we do?

And nobody—no freelancer, no staff writer, no producer—nobody ever came in and said, "I've got a story," and pitched it. Everything was pitched in the room. And when a story is being pitched and formed and all that sort of thing, at some point—in the early stages—you would get assigned it or another writer would get assigned it. That was the way it worked.

What did you learn about story in that process?

Phoef Sutton: Well, I mean, you learned everything.

I mean, obviously the stories for a sitcom, particularly a sitcom like *Cheers*, are fairly simple: There's a problem that's presented. Halfway through, it takes a turn and then it's resolved. *[LAUGHS]* And usually—for the first five years of the show—it's getting resolved involved something to do with Diane, because she was pivotal.

But I think more what I learned was that when you're first a writer and you write something—and it's good, it's bad, whatever—you generally think, "Well, that's it, that's what it is, and I can't come up with anything else. That's what it is."

And when people give you notes or object to it, you resist the notes. And the main reason you resist the notes, I think, is that you can't think how to change it. You can't figure out anything different. And I just learned very early on that there's always a different way to do something. Anything, anything. Nothing is perfect. Everything—always—has a different way to go. There's always a different way to look at it. Always a different approach to take to it.

And maybe that approach won't be better. Maybe it'll be a linear move. Maybe it'll be worse. On *Cheers*, it was almost always better. It almost always got better. I'd say it always got better in the room.

Cheers is well known for—unlike other series where major cast members left—you guys handled it better than anyone ever. Do you have any idea what was the magic powder that made it work where you guys did it?

Phoef Sutton: Well, there were a couple of things. First of all, the cast always changed. The cast was always changing. It was never the same. I mean, there were the people who were replaced, left and were replaced. But there were also the people who came in. Frasier, Lilith.

One of the reasons the show lasted as long as it did was that when you were writing, if you were writing year eight, it was a way different show from when we were writing year three. A very different cast.

I'd say the biggest thing that I learned—and I got to do this, because on *Chesapeake Shores*, we lost the star of the show too, and I had to replace him—was just to make the character as different as possible from the one you're replacing. So that nobody thinks, "Oh, this guy isn't as good as that guy," or, "This girl is not the same thing as that."

When Coach died and they brought in Woody, there was still the dumb aspect of him. But in general, he was a very different character. He was a young character. He was a naive character. He was from the Midwest. Whereas Coach had been from Sam's life, and he was a ball player, and he was kind of old and kind of brain damaged from getting hit in the head with balls. And they were very different.

When Rebecca came in, they made her a completely different character. And one of the reasons they were able to do that was, I think, just luck. Because they had the character of Frasier. And so much of the show was the intellectual versus the blue-collar type people. And Frasier was able to take that on. He had already taken it on from Diane, but he was able to take that on entirely.

So, the new character didn't have to be an intellectual type, snobby type. What was originally intended was a hard-nosed businessman who clashed with Sam. It didn't actually turn out that way. She turned out to be more of a basket case, but that was because of the actress and playing to the actress's strengths.

And that, I think, is the main thing I learned from that. Because really, when Diane left the show, the show had been on for five years, which is the run of most shows. No show had really survived the loss of its star and she really was the star. I mean, she was the pivotal point of every episode. She was the one, the audience was coming into the bar and seeing it through her eyes. Ted was certainly the costar, but she was really the focal point of the show. So, when she left, we were really scared. We did not know whether it was going to work.

And the show shifted then, because it became much more of an ensemble show, because Kirstie—although she was a wonderful actress—she wasn't quite the dominant force that Shelley Long had been. The show really became about Sam and the bar. It had been moving that way already, but it became that way.

If you were to describe the show when it first started, it would surely have been: it's a love story between Sam and Diane and will they get together or not? And then it became a show about a bar, about the patrons of a bar and their lives.

What prompted your transition from TV writing to novel writing? Was there a significant event?

Phoef Sutton: No, I'd always wanted to write novels. I'd always wanted to. And I saw myself approaching 40 and thought, "Well, I'm going to do it." And so, I just started doing it. I wrote a couple, not really even thinking that they would get published, but just to see what it was like. And they got published and it's been a great thing.

I mean, you don't make any money at it. *[LAUGHS]* I mean, Janet Evanovich and John Grisham and Robert Patterson do, but most people don't make money at it. It's really a labor of love.

But you get tired of the network notes. And you get tired of writing with other people. And you can do it by yourself.

Now, I do miss writing with other people. I go back to television occasionally because it's great to look at somebody and say, "Well, what do you think? Well, you come up with something?"

You don't have to come up with everything. But you do in a book.

So, was *Always Six O'Clock* the first novel? Or just the first published one?

Phoef Sutton: It was the first novel I wrote.

And what did you do? I read the later version, *15 Minutes To Live*. How did you change that?

Phoef Sutton: Well, actually it was sort of the other way around. *15 Minutes To Live* was the original version of the novel.

Despite the fact that you think you don't get notes in writing a novel, you do get notes. I was influenced to change it in ways that I later regretted. And so, I wanted to publish it by myself. It hadn't sold well. It was a long time afterward that I wrote [the publisher] and tried to get the rights back so that I could self-publish it myself. And they finally gave it to me. And I self-published it. And then it was published by Brash Books. It's nice to have it out there as I originally intended it to be.

So, the version I read, which was 2015, was what you intended. And the earlier version was what they made you change it to.

Phoef Sutton: Yeah. I mean, they didn't make me. I probably listened to the notes too much, because I was used to listening to notes. I haven't run into that so much since then.

Did your work as a TV writer make it easier for you to do that first novel?

Phoef Sutton: I always say that when it comes down to it, every form of writing—at least fiction writing—whether it's a playwright, whether you're writing an hour drama, whether you're writing a half hour comedy for television, whether you're writing a screenplay, whether you're writing a novel: it basically comes down to writing scenes. To writing good scenes between people where they want something from each other.

And that was a constant; that has stayed true. So, in that sense, my experience of doing that made it easier. Obviously in a novel, you also get to go inside people's heads and say what they're thinking, which is a great advantage. You can't do that in a screenplay or play or a movie, unless you have voiceover. But you can only do that so much.

But still, you don't want to do that <u>that</u> much. Basically, you want to show, not tell—as they say—with all of those forms.

The biggest difference was that it takes tremendously longer to write a novel. I mean, you can write a half hour comedy, if your back's to the wall, you can write a half hour comedy in a night. You can certainly write one in a week.

You can write an hour drama in a week, or two weeks. A screenplay in a month or two months. A novel, it's hard to do it in less than six months. And even that's pretty fast. I think it was E. L. Doctorow who said it's like driving down a highway at night. You can see in front of you with the headlights, but there's all that behind you and all that in front of you that you can't see.

And it's very hard to hold it all in your head. You can hold a half hour comedy in your head with no problem. And even an hour drama, you can compartmentalize the four acts and kind of do that. With a screenplay, you can almost do it.

With a novel, forget it. You can't do it. You can't do it. It's just too much. And my novels are not terribly long. I don't write like *Game of Thrones*. But still, it's hard.

You had a lot of experience with character, a lot of experi-

ence with dialogue, with scenes. Was prose a difficult part for you to figure out what to say and how much of it to say?

Phoef Sutton: How to write in complete sentences? *[LAUGHS]* Yeah, you have to adjust your thinking.

I think Elmore Leonard, one of his rules of writing is: don't write the parts that people skip over when they read it.

So, I don't write long descriptions of nature. I mean, I'll do it occasionally if it seems important. But basically, I just describe what you need to describe.

But what you need to describe is all the stuff that when you're writing a screenplay or a television play, you figure, "Well, the art director is going to take care of the room," and, "The costumer is going to take care of the costumes," and "The photographer is going to take care of the way it looks."

You're all of those things as a writer. You have to describe enough of what they're wearing to get an idea of who they are. Not go into a lengthy fashion discourse. And you have to describe enough of the setting that you know what it is. Yeah, that's tough. That is tough.

But you obviously figured it out.

Phoef Sutton: I guess I did. I mean, I don't know. *[LAUGHS]* A lot of writers say this, but, whenever you look at the blank page or the blank screen and you have to start something off, you basically feel like you don't know anything. You've been fooling people all along and they're finally going to realize you don't know how to write. It's always a struggle to start.

How did you get involved in Lee Goldberg's *Dead Man* series? And what was that like, working into an existing series?

Phoef Sutton: Well, again, it was a lot like writing for a [TV] series. When I got on *Boston Legal*, I just tried to write like the original writer was writing it but bring my own touch to it. And that's one of the special skills you have to learn as a television writer if you're on a show: How to write for that show but bring your own voice to it. It's tricky.

I met Lee at a writer's conference that was in Pasadena at one time. And we just hit it off, and we've been good friends ever since. And he came to me with that. I always have been a fan of and loved genre fiction, horror fiction, horror movies, genre movies. But I've never really written that sort of thing before, and never really written it since either. I don't know why. I'm surprised. Maybe because I really like it, but it was fun. It was fun.

The idea of that was, it was a series of short novels that were about the same character linked together, that different writers wrote. It was supposed to be like a television series, but novels. And it didn't quite work. It didn't quite sell as well as we'd hoped, but it was a good try.

Was that the same sort of technique you use when you work with Janet Evanovich?

Phoef Sutton: Yeah, yeah.

Are you trying to imitate and sound like her?

Phoef Sutton: Oh yeah, more so in that case, because they were her books, they were her series. So yeah, but I think my tone is fairly humorous but serious. And that's her tone too. So, we're a pretty good match.

You're the only one I know who really has taken that—working in episodic TV, different series—taking that same mindset and working with other writers on their series. And

it is, I think, a unique gift you have, because *Boston Legal* is quite different than *Cheers*, which is quite different than the *Bob Newhart* show. And yet you're able to adapt to all of them, and you're doing the same thing with these books.

Phoef Sutton: Yeah, well, I guess that's one of my talents. I wrote for *Terriers*. And when I started writing for *Chesapeake Shores*, all the actors said I got their voices really well. So, it's just something that I can do. I don't quite know how to teach it to anyone.

And an asterisk here about *Terriers*: What a great series. And why isn't that still running today?

Phoef Sutton: We were surprised. *[LAUGHS]* We shot all the show before it aired. And we were expecting to be quite the hit. And FX—we were always telling ourselves that FX doesn't cancel stuff—so we'll get a chance regardless. They decided to cancel stuff that year. It was a disappointment, because that was a really fun show to work on and a great show.

And a really fun show to watch. Okay, Let's talk about *Crush*, because that's my favorite of your novels. Where did *Crush* come from?

Phoef Sutton: Well, actually *Crush* was originally a pilot that I wrote. And then it was a screenplay that I wrote. And then I turned it into a novel. Because I got tired of writing screenplays, ad nauseum, then they never get made, because that's the life of a screenwriter.

And most of the screenwriting that I had done had been based on other things. So I couldn't do anything with them because it was based on another project. But that one was an original one.

One of the problems I had with *15 Minutes to Live* was that people couldn't tell exactly what it was. Was it a thriller? Was it a romance? Was it a ...? And I thought, well, I'm going to write something that's definitely a genre book. It's clearly hard-boiled fiction. And I just took [the script] and adapted it into a book.

I really liked the character. The character was nothing like me, unlike the character in *15 Minutes to Live* and other characters that I have written. He was basically nothing like me. But I just thought a big, strong, tough, good guy would be an interesting approach. You know, a strong silent type.

The word you left out in describing it was *funny*, because it's also a very funny book, even though it's all those other things.

Phoef Sutton: If I try to write the most serious book I could think of it would end up being funny. I just look at life that way. I have had tragedies and difficult times in my life, and I could always find the funny side of it. Life's like that, you know?

I'm not surprised in you saying that the first *Crush* book was based on a screenplay. It has a very cinematic quality to it, and it has a pace to it, but they all do.

What did you learn about pace in writing for television? Because you've written, just comparing *Cheers* in front of a live audience with *Boston Legal*, which is a one camera drama. You certainly have figured out pace on TV. How were you able to adapt that to novel writing?

Phoef Sutton: All I can say is that every scene has to fulfill a purpose in telling the story. There has to be a reason for every scene to be there. And if that reason is strong enough, it holds the interest of the audience.

And that's really the main thing. You don't want to do a scene that you think if you cut that scene, it wouldn't matter. You have to ramp up the tension, then you have to let it down, and all that. That stuff you'll learn, too. But the main thing is just to know why that scene is there, and what to do to communicate the purpose of that scene.

The first *Crush* book was based on a screenplay; in subsequent books, are you working from an outline?

Phoef Sutton: I work from a loose outline. You know, in movies and TV, you have to outline. You have to outline in great detail. And, partially, you have to outline for the network and the studio. But also, you have to outline for the production staff, for everybody. Everybody has to know what's coming next. So, you have to write really detailed outlines.

I kind of liked not writing really detailed outlines for the books, just because it was different. I sort of roughly outlined the thing, leaving the end kind of up in the air. Because you never know how it's going to end, and you never know what's going to be different from what you thought. You maybe have a different idea of who did it, if it's a whodunit, or whatever. Then you go back and change things to set that up.

I like Lee Childs. I guess, he begins his books, and he has no idea where it's going and just writes it. And that works for him. I don't do that. But at the same time, I'll do a loose outline and I leave myself free to deviate from it when I think of something better.

How do you think your years writing dialogue that has to be spoken by actors helps you write dialogue for the page?

Phoef Sutton: It's vitally important. Knowing that, knowing the way people sound, the cadence of individual characters, and the way they talk—and all that—is great. I mean, you have to realize that when you're writing a book, they aren't going to hear an actor saying it. But I think they kind of hear it in their minds.

You mentioned the difference between writing for a Kelsey Grammer versus a James Spader versus a Ted Danson. You seem to have the gift to do that. And I'm guessing that somehow that translates when you sit down to write a novel.

Phoef Sutton: Yeah. I mean, if you have an idea of who the character is, then they will know. And hopefully you can write it so that you don't have to write "Sam said" after every line. You can write it until you kind of hear the individual people's voices within your head.

So, when you sit down to start a novel, are there any tools or tricks that you're bringing to the process that you know you got from working in TV all those years?

Phoef Sutton: Panic. Fear. *[LAUGHS]* You want to have an initial moment that gets people interested: either curious about what happens, or that it's funny or that it grabs people, and they want to keep reading.

And I find the hardest part of anything is the start of it. I will often write into a show first, into a script first, or into a book first. I'll write one of the later scenes first, and then go back and write the beginning later. And I almost always change the beginning myriad times. That's the thing that changes most. Because until you've written quite a bit of a book, I don't really know what it's about. I don't really know what its theme is.

And so, I often go back and rewrite the beginning to lead into it in a more appropriate way. As a matter of fact, when I'm writing scripts, I often—because I've outlined it in detail—I'll often write it scattershot: write the fifth scene first, and then the eighth scene, then the twelfth scene, then go back and write the third scene.

And then I do that a lot. I don't know very many people who do that.

It's your unique method. So, for aspiring novelists who don't have the history of writing for TV that you do, is there one piece of advice you'd want to give them based on your experience? Something that might help them in their novel writing?

Phoef Sutton: Just keep writing. Just keep writing every day. Write something every day. Ray Bradbury used to say, "Write a short story a day." I could never do that. But just keep at it because you will get better. You will get better at it.

I think there's a really good lesson in your story about your first year on *Cheers*, where you didn't say much, and you just absorbed. I don't know exactly how that applies to novel writers...

Phoef Sutton: Well, I think, I think it applies to everyone in the world right now. I think the world would be greatly improved if people didn't say so much. People talk way too much.

You know, there's that old saying, I don't know who said it, Mark Twain or whoever: "Better to be silent and thought a fool than to speak up and prove it." Just don't talk. *[LAUGHS]* Just take it in. Be the strong, silent type. *[LAUGHS]*

Be like Crush.

Phoef Sutton: Yeah. Yeah. Be like Crush. I wish I was like Crush. *[LAUGHS]*

ELLEN BYRON

Ellen Byron is a true multi-hyphenate talent whose work spans novels, television, plays, and more. While originally intending to pursue acting after getting her theater degree, Byron found her calling as a writer instead. She first made her mark in the theater world as an award-winning playwright. Byron then transitioned to television writing, racking up credits on hit sitcoms like Wings, Just Shoot Me!, and The Fairly OddParents over a prolific 25-year career. Her ability to craft pitch-perfect comedic dialogue and memorable characters served her well on the small screen.

More recently, Byron turned her talents to novel writing and has garnered major acclaim. Her Cajun Country Mysteries have nabbed multiple Agatha and Lefty awards for Best Contemporary and Best Humorous Mystery. The first book in her new Vintage Cookbook Mystery series, Bayou Book Thief, was nominated for an Anthony Award.

One key insight Byron offers is the importance of always remaining open to learning and growing as a writer, no matter how much experience you accumulate. As she puts it: "Be a lifetime learner...An openness to learning will improve your writing and make it more interesting for you as well as for the reader."

Let's start with a little bit of background. Did you plan on being a writer?

Ellen Byron: No, I was going to be an actress. I got my degree in theater. I went to New York. I actually did some commercial work, plays and some summer stock and stuff And then I joined Actors Equity, but I wasn't getting work. So, to kill time, I started writing.

I wrote a play for my friends to do. And I got a reading and my friends all sucked playing themselves. But I really liked the writing. So, I transitioned. I remember I ran into an actor-turned-playwright, Jim McClure—who wrote a play called *Lone Star* and I knew him from our mutual world—and he said, "Oh, so you're a writer now?" I said, "No, I'm still a performer." And he goes, "Oh, that'll go away."

But what happened is that at around the same time—I started writing plays in the early eighties—I got involved with an improv company that was just starting up. It's called Theater Sports, and it's inspired by Keith Johnstone, who passed away recently. He wrote a book called *Impro*. He was British, but then he ended up in Calgary. And he started this form of quote unquote "competitive improv." You did it in teams, but the whole point was to give you the chance to fail and to take big leaps and risks. Because if it was bad, you'd be pulled off stage. It was about creating story and not Bar-prov (as he called it), where it's just jokes and people trying to one up each other.

So as my writing career started, I was doing that (improv) to kind of scratch the performing itch. And I think they worked really well together, because it's all about teamwork.

And then I decided to write for television. I literally remember the moment. I'd gotten a reading of one of my plays at Circle Rep. It was a full-length play, it was a finalist at the O'Neill and it didn't make it. But I kept getting these readings. And I still remember: I was in my New York apartment, getting notes from the guy who ran the workshop program. And I thought, "God, if I'm going to be taking notes, somebody should pay me to take them." And that's when I decided I should go into television.

So, you decide if you're going to be taking notes, you might as well get paid for it. You decide TV is the way to go. That's great, but how do you then make it happen that you write for TV?

Ellen Byron: First, I would watch sitcoms. Some of them were terrible.

This was like the late 1980s. But I literally studied how they were structured. And then I took a couple of classes in New York before I came here. And the guy who was teaching them —it was good. I mean, I learned stuff. I don't know what his background was, but at one point he said, "You know, I got into a little trouble gambling, so I have to leave for a while." And then he disappeared. He literally left. I don't know whatever happened to him, but he had to make a run for it.

And I finally decided that if I was really going to pursue it, I had to move to Los Angeles, which is really hard. Because I never imagined living anywhere but New York. I'm a native New Yorker. I went to school in New Orleans, which was fabulous. And I loved it. And now New York and New Orleans duke it out for my favorite city. Which is ironic, since I've lived in LA for over 30 years now, and I'm forcing myself to really appreciate it more and more.

I got in touch with the UCLA Writers Extension Program about possibly teaching playwriting class. And so, I was teaching like one night a week or on a Saturday, a full day workshop. And I got a free class with every semester I taught, so I would use that. I was taking some sitcom classes. And because I had theater agents in New York, I was able to get some agents out here. But they were not at the level I needed to really break in.

And then in one of the classes I met another woman, and we were assigned to each other as buddies in an Advanced Sitcom Lab. We respected each other's work, and so we began writing scripts together.

So, I moved out here in April of 1990. And got my first TV job with my writing partner in June of 1992.

What was that first job?

Ellen Byron: It was a show called *Flying Blind*. It was with Tea Leoni. And it was a very, very quirky show. Ritchie Rosenstock had his very unique structure for jokes. In fact, one of his friends who worked on the pilot and then came to some of the episodes we were shooting, said, "How does it feel to be writing jokes you won't be able to use anywhere else?"

So, was there a point where things clicked for you, and you had a clear understanding of how to structure and write a TV script?

Ellen Byron: I think that happened before. We had to write good, really strong spec scripts to get read and then hired. So, I trained myself before we actually got on staff. I knew what the structure was and how to write it before someone was paying me to do it.

Did the process of needing to write outlines for TV scripts, did that help you when you switched to novel writing?

Ellen Byron: Oh, absolutely. I still to this day do not understand how people pants books. To me, it's like, that seems to be magic.

I actually just wrote a short story and I thought, "Oh, well then, I'll be able to pants it now." And it literally was like my brain was bursting until I finally just wrote down the outline of what I need to do and where I need to go.

There's Pantsers and Plotters. I actually have pushed back a lot. I created a workshop I've done a couple of places. I call it, The Organics of Outlining, because my position is that outlining is every bit as organic. It's just at a different point in the process.

I was doing this workshop somewhere and a woman said, "Oh, so like your outline is kind of like your first draft." And I thought, "Oh my gosh, that's so great because it's absolutely true." And I think when people get resistant and terrified of outlining, I think what they think is that it's like chiseled into stone and you can't move it.

I'm working on a thing right now, an outline. I usually end up with around a 30-page single spaced outline and it's broken down into chapters. Well, the chapters have completely changed. And as I'm writing, I see, "Wait, this makes no sense. I'm repeating myself." Or, "Oh, I'm missing this." So, I call my outlines *fluid outlines.*

And look, I hated writing outlines for the TV shows. It's like this, you're doing two things simultaneously [PATS STOMACH AND RUBS HEAD]: You're laying out a story, but an outline has to be funny. It can't be straight.

Look, there are people I met occasionally, I'd meet these TV writers who say, "Well, you know, I get a good solid script down. And then the room will punch it up." I'm like, "No, that means you're going to have a very short career," because if you cannot lay out a story and make it funny, you will not work.

Nobody wants to go, "Oh, this is very good, and we don't care if it doesn't have jokes. That's our job." No, it's everyone's job to make it funnier, but it has to be there to begin with. Otherwise, you're just slogging through.

It's punishing. I worked on mostly network sitcoms—some cable—but it's a very punishing schedule. And so, the stronger that first draft is, the greater the favor you're doing for the show.

In TV, creating the outline isn't optional. That's part of your pay structure.

Ellen Byron: Well, that's what I tell people. I say, "That's why I do it. It's the pay structure." If you're doing a pilot or something, you get paid for commencement, outline, first draft, second draft, and a polish.

So, it's probably built into your muscle memory to always start a story with an outline.

Ellen Byron: Yes. And also, I think because my brain gets ahead of itself, I need to write down. When I start laying things out and seeing what's going to happen, I need to write that down. And then it becomes an outline.

I'm just in awe of people. I don't know how they do it. They're just kind of like, "Well, I sat down, and I had a man and a woman and, you know, thirty pages later, I had a fabulous relationship." I'm like, "What? How did you do that?"

Look, I think we all have to find the way to write that works for us. There's no—as I always tell people—there's no right or wrong, there's only what works for you. I heard James Elroy— and I've said this a million times—I heard James Elroy speak once, and he said he wrote an outline for a book that was 720 pages. The outline was longer than the book. And I was like, "No, I'd kill myself. I could never do that."

So, at what point—you'd gone from acting to playwriting to TV writing—when did you make the switch into novel writing and what was it that inspired that leap?

Ellen Byron: Unemployment. A TV writer's career is up and down. If you get like the evergreen credit—like *Friends* or *Frasier*—you can just ride that out to retirement. If you don't have that credit, it's catch as catch can. And a lot of it is based on hype.

And also—in the 1990s when my writing partner and I came up —it was like, "Oh, we need women." And so, there'd be the token women's slot. If I wrote a memoir—which I have no intention of ever doing—I would call it, *"They Have Their Woman: My Life in Hollywood."* Because I can't tell you how many times we'd say to our agent, "We heard from friends this show is looking." And he or she would say, "Oh, they have their woman." So, we were having trouble getting work.

I loved reading mysteries and so—remember how I said I would get a free class when I taught? In 1999, I was pregnant, and I was teaching during the summer. It was another lull— another forced work hiatus—so I took a mystery writing class as my free class. A writer we had worked with on a show back-stabbed us and I wanted to kill him. I couldn't do it in real life, so I thought, "Well, I'll write a mystery."

And what I realized was—although I was the only professional writer in the class—what I was writing wasn't as good as what the other people were writing. So, I thought, "Oh, I can't do this."

Cut to: Eleven years later. A friend of mine had started a very small little writers' group for four of us. And I thought, "Well,

I'm going to try writing a mystery again, because that's what I love to read." And I had the time, because I wasn't working.

I knew nothing about these conventions and conferences. I'd never heard of any of them. But there was a writer named Denise Hamilton and she mentioned she was going to Thriller Fest. And I thought, "Well, is there anything like that if you're not writing thrillers?" And she mentioned Malice Domestic, and I looked into it. I saw on the website they had a grant and I applied for it. I was one of the two winners at the time. The other was Renee Patrick, which is Rosemarie and Vince Keena, writing as a team.

But that book never sold. It took me nine months to get an agent, which is unusual. I've had agents or managers since I was in my twenties. So that was quite humbling. And I realized why: that particular manuscript was a little too jaded to be a full-on cozy. It wasn't quite a traditional, so I think that's why.

But anyway, Doug—who's now been my agent since then—he liked it. He said, "I'll take a chance." And while it was on submission, I just was bored. And so, I wrote *Plantation Shutters*. And that did sell.

We were doing pilots and for four years it was like a pilot ... and no work ... a pilot. And then in 2014 simultaneously *Plantation Shutters* sold to Crooked Lane and my writing partner and I got a job on *Fairly Odd Parents*.

The good thing was that animation operates very differently than live action. And so, it was the first time I actually worked for a corporation. When you're working on a show, you're working for the production company. *Fairly Odd Parents* was on Nickelodeon, so I was actually working directly with Nickelodeon.

[With animation] the coming together of the writing and the art all takes place over a much more extended period of time. The hours were much more like having a regular job. So, I could write. And I wrote the second and third Cajun Country books while I was working at Nickelodeon on *Fairly Odd Parents* and then *Bunsen is a Beast*.

When you made the transition into writing novels, having worked with a partner for so long, what was the upside and the downside of doing it on your own?

Ellen Byron: You know, I'd started on my own as a playwright. The upside was that I got to do whatever I wanted. And that was very freeing. And I think she would say the same thing, because she actually stayed in animation and she's doing animation now.

And I remember one of our bosses said, "You know, usually with a team, one person is better at story, one person is better at jokes. But you guys are great at both of them." And I think we had a reputation as strong first draft writers, because we had the two of us breaking the story and punching it up. You had, you know, two people.

And that was really important to be able to say we're strong first draft writers and then have our bosses from different shows back that up. I mean, I remember we worked on a show called *It's All Relative* and the schedule got really, really tight. And we wrote an episode where the showrunner said, "We're just taking this right to the table. We're not even going to bother to do a punch up on it." And I was like, "Oh, my God, that never ever happens."

So, she (my writing partner) didn't read or write mysteries and that was fine. And I did start to get involved with Sisters in Crime and The Guppies and I found some friends and we became each other's beta readers. I feel like I'm also my own beta reader on some level now. And I have editors who will give me real notes. But, you know, I've been earning my living as a writer now—if you count the teaching within that—for forty years.

You mentioned briefly about getting notes. How did your experience in television and receiving notes help you when you're writing novels and getting notes?

Ellen Byron: I learned early on when I was writing plays that you have to distill notes. I made a big, big mistake early on in my career. I'd written a play, and I was part of a writer's group. One of the playwrights in it who was much more established said, "Well, I think this would work better if it was a <u>father</u> and daughter, you know, make it more immediate."

And I was like, "Oh, okay, great. You're right." So, I rewrote the play with the father and daughter. But I was writing his play, not my play. And what I realized early on was that there are notes, and then there's playwriting, which is people telling you how <u>they</u> would write your book or play or script.

And you really have to learn to hear the essence of a note. And not necessarily take it literally. On several shows I worked on— especially with one particular showrunner who I worked with a couple of times—the network would give notes and he'd be like, "We should do that."

And I'd go, "No, no, no, no, no, no. If we do that, we're going to have to throw out the whole thing. Don't take it literally. They're making suggestions, but they're not writers. What is the essence of the note?"

I remember my writing partner and I had written a pilot for NBC. David Nevins—who I loved. He was one of my favorite executives. He ended up running Showtime and doing a whole bunch of great stuff. He was a really cool guy. I liked him a lot. So, we sat down with him, and he said, "I really, really like this pilot. This is going to be a very short meeting. I just have one note."

And he gave the note. And you're sitting there with these top-level network people. And I said, "Okay, well, David, we can absolutely do that. Just so you know, you said you really liked this pilot, but if we take that note, we will have to throw out the second act. And we are happy to do that. If that's what you want."

He was like, "No, no, I don't want you to do that." So, what was supposed to be a short meeting with one note turned into like an hour and a half of us brainstorming about how we could solve his note and protect what he liked.

And so, I think the training as a playwright, the training working in TV, learning to distill and get to the essence of a note, is very important. Because you could end up with something that's a complete hodgepodge if you're trying to serve every master.

A lot of people pitch stuff and it's like, they're not thinking that it's like pulling a thread. They don't think, "Oh, if you do that, then the dominoes all fall."

And that's a great point: Are they trying to fix their story? Or are they trying to fix your story?

Ellen Byron: Right. And that's what you get so much from other writers, when you get network or studio notes. I mean, a lot of times, they're just thinking off the top of their head, because they have a problem and they think, "Well, maybe this will be the solution." But it's not necessarily an order.

A writer I worked with used to call some notes "bay leaves," because of the way you put a bay leaf in and then you take it out. A lot of times, we would occasionally do that on the script.

You mentioned writing pilots. You've currently got three different novel series running. And you've talked in the past about setting up your series of books like you would set up a TV series. And that the first book is the pilot. Can you dive into the mechanics of thinking that way when you're writing that first book in what you hope will be a series?

Ellen Byron: You're introducing the world and the characters to readers. And so, there's a lot of what we call laying pipe. You're building the foundation of what the series will be. So, you're laying the pipe. And sometimes it's easier than others.

I also think that often a series actually gets better as it goes along. The same is true of TV series. I mean, if you look at the pilots for *Frasier*, for *Friends*, or some of the biggest hits, or for *Seinfeld*, you go, "Wow, this show got so much better."

How much planning ahead are you doing when it comes to first book in a series as relates to a pilot of a TV series? I'm sure we both read or seen TV pilots where you watched it and went, "They have no idea what happens next. They sold an interesting idea, but they have no idea."

Ellen Byron: You know, it's so funny, I knew someone when *Lost* was on the air. I was working on a show and there was a writer's assistant on the show. We were both obsessed with it. And he was great. We were like, "Are they making it up? It feels like they're making it up as they go, but maybe they have this amazing grand plan."

And he said, "I talked to writers' assistants on the show. They're making it up. They're totally making it up as they go."

And you'll see that when a character *pops* who was supposed to be a day player. There's a famous story with Drew Carey that Kathy Kinney was only supposed to be in the pilot. But she and Drew had such a great dynamic that she became a series regular.

Chemistry is always more obvious with actors. It's just in your face. But in a book, I think it becomes 'what is fun to write to?'

How far ahead are you planning, series-wise?

Ellen Byron: There are the very vaguest of benchmarks. For example, in The Cajun Country Mystery Series, I knew that eventually I wanted her to get married, and eventually have a child.

When I'm pitching a series, you have to lay out plots for the first three books, usually. My agent always says, do five or six. So, by even the third, fourth, or fifth, I'm like, just pulling it out of my ass. And sometimes you get there and go, "Oh!"

I'm dealing with that right now. It's like I realized in two of my series, I've either borrowed from that story for something else or it doesn't really track. So, I'll have to start from scratch. But as you create the characters in the world, new ideas pop up for you.

People say, "Well, do you do a three episode, a three-book arc?" I always say 'episode.' I tend to talk in TV terms. I don't say plot and subplot, I say A story, B story, Runner. It's so ingrained in me.

Can you talk a little bit about the differences in writing dialogue in plays versus TV versus novels?

Ellen Byron: What I learned as a playwright—and this holds true in every form of fiction writing, I believe—is that the dramaturg or the director, whoever's reading it, should know who's talking without having to look at the character name.

And what that means is that you've created unique voices for each of your characters. I think that's true in every kind of good writing. If you look at *Big Bang Theory*, that show is really funny. And I give it major props for doing something that is very rare —and they did it on *Friends*, too—where you create three women with different comic points of view.

They did do that on *Friends*. Although in the first season, you could tell they struggled to find where Courtney Cox was funny. There's a scene in the first season where they literally just did reaction shots from her. And I knew why. It's because whatever lines they gave her didn't work. And then, finally, they realized that Courtney—in real life—is kind of anal about cleaning and stuff. And so, they wrote to that as her character, and it worked out fine.

But if you look at a show, a really good sitcom—like *Big Bang* or *Will & Grace* or *Friends*—each of those characters has a very distinctive comic voice. And when you're writing these shows, it helps you write to those characters if you know what their comic voice is.

It's a little harder to do in books, because in a sitcom you're really creating a joke structure for each character in the best of the sitcoms. *Seinfeld* is a very specific structure.

People are more just talking in a book. But there's still a way of getting their character across. If you have a character who's self-involved, well, that'll work into their dialogue. If you have a character who's anal, well, you work that into their dialogue. I think in any form of literature, you have to find unique voices for all of your characters. And then have that come out in the dialogue. And it has to sound natural.

Did it help for you in playwriting and in TV writing that you'd write something and then you'd hear somebody say it and you could learn from that?

Ellen Byron: Probably. I guess. I don't really know. Maybe it was from the acting. I don't know. I mean, I think yes. I mean, you could really see it on its feet. In TV of course, when you work on a good show—and the voices are very clearly defined —you're writing specific jokes and dialogue for that particular character. It really becomes ingrained in you.

It's also getting into their behavior. That's one thing you can do. It's not just dialogue, it's behavior. It's using behavior to illustrate the character along with dialogue.

What did writing for TV teach you about act breaks and how you incorporated that thinking into writing chapters and novels?

Ellen Byron: You want to engage people and feel like they have to learn what happens next. And that's something I learned in improv, too. We used to do an improv called What Happens Next, and it's all about building story. And so that really applied very well to writing a sitcom and to writing books. What happens next? How do you engage people?

And so, in every chapter, I follow the same thing, where it ends on a story beat that will propel people into the next chapter.

I have some pretty heavy B stories in my books, but I always try to marry the A and the B story, eventually have them influence each other. So sometimes, once the book is going, I will end on the plot point for the B story instead of the A story. But I usually wait to let things really start chugging along before I do that. Because you don't want people to go to the refrigerator or start channel surfing. You want to make sure they stick around because they have to, because they want to know what happens next.

That idea prompted another thought: It's something I know that I do when I'm writing. And I know you do it naturally, but people might not be thinking about it. It's the idea that you're not just writing in a novel, probably not writing one story. You're writing one main story, but you have to have branches to go to. I mean, even if you go into *To Kill a Mockingbird*, there's a main story, but there's also branching stories, right?

I think you probably are naturally creating that when you do your outline. Your mind just goes, "That's not enough. I'm going to need another thing." Was that something you learned in TV, that you couldn't just have an A story?

Ellen Byron: Well, yes. As I say, "There are a lot of mouths to feed." When you're working on a show like *Wings*, you have eight or nine regular characters who all need funny stuff. And you cannot squeeze them all into an A story. The A scenes of a *Wings* episode were backbreaking because you had to make sure everyone was in them. You had to launch every story and they had to be funny. So, you have to know when to balance, when something takes precedence and something else doesn't and go back and forth.

My goal is—and I don't always achieve it—but my goal is to always integrate: at some point what she's doing for the B story is going to tie into the A story and help her discover the most important clue of all.

And then there are runners. There are things you have as runners. And things that seem like runners, and then suddenly pay off.

There's nothing better in a mystery than when a runner turns out to be important, and you had no idea all along. It's such a delight, as a writer, when you stumble onto those things.

So finally, for aspiring novelists out there, is there one piece of advice that you'd give them about novel writing based on what you've learned both as a novelist and a TV writer?

Ellen Byron: I think it's—of course—write.

But also, I think it's be a lifetime learner. You may reach a point of saturation in terms of taking too many classes, but always be open to learning new things and letting them influence your work. That's exciting. An openness to learning will improve your writing and make it more interesting for you as well as for the reader.

JOHN AUGUST

John August is a highly accomplished and versatile writer who has found major success across film, television, theater, and novels. He first made his mark as a screenwriter, penning iconic movies like <u>Go,</u> following that up with several collaborations with director Tim Burton, including <u>Big Fish,</u> <u>Corpse Bride,</u> <u>Charlie and The Choco-</u><u>late Factory,</u> and <u>Frankenweenie.</u>

While continuing to write for the big screen, August has also transitioned to other mediums in recent years. He wrote the book for the Broadway musical adaptation of his film <u>Big Fish,</u> And he created the popular <u>Arlo Finch</u> middle-grade novel series, drawing from his own experiences as a Boy Scout to craft a magical world that has resonated with young readers.

In addition to everything else, August also co-hosts the wildly popular <u>Scriptnotes</u> podcast with Craig Mazin, where they discuss the craft of screenwriting and how to navigate the film industry. The long-running show is an invaluable resource for writers at all levels.

One insight August offered in our chat is the value of constantly challenging yourself as a writer by working in new formats and genres. As he puts it: "It was nice feeling like a beginner again...I wanted to challenge myself and it was nice not being an expert in something." This growth mindset has allowed August to avoid creative stagnation throughout his prolific career.

First, a little background. Was it always going to be screenwriting? Was it always going to be writing?

John August: It was always going to be writing. I didn't know that there was such a thing as screenwriting until sometime in early college—when I first read a screenplay. I read the screenplay for *Sex, Lies, & Videotape*, which was published as a book. And so, I could read that with a movie. It's like, oh, that's actually how it all works.

But I had always been writing. I'd written short stories. I had a journalism degree, so I was always going to do some form of writing. I was praised for it early on and I'm a praise-seeking creature.

And you went to school for it, didn't you?

John August: Yeah, my degree was in journalism. It's an advertising focused degree at Drake University. And I liked it. I did sort of magazine journalism too. If I hadn't gotten into USC for film school, I probably would have headed East and try to do magazine journalism.

And what was your USC experience like?

John August: It was good. So, I was in the two-year Peter Stark program, which is the producer's program. We read a ton of scripts, which was by far the most helpful thing. We had a great script library there. We could check out scripts. We were also reading what was in production, what was in development. We were reading a ton. We were reading a ton of stuff. And you just get a sense of your own taste and what works for you.

It was while I was there that I wrote *X*, which became the first part of *Go*. I finished my first script that summer between the two years. That got me an agent and sort of got the process started.

I remember from the podcast, you mentioned that you did some work at Universal. What was that involving?

John August: I was an intern there. I was interning in my summer between the two years. I was just in physical production, so I was the person who filed the budgets and things like that. The first half of the summer was just really mindless paperwork that required no brain cells. So, when I'd come home at night, I would write—handwrite pages—and then I would type them up during lunch. And so, I actually got a lot done that summer.

I ended up also doing clearances, which is anything that shows up on screen that somebody could own the copyright to, making sure you had clearance to actually put that up on the screen.

You worked professionally as a screenwriter for quite a while before you wrote *Arlo Finch*. What was the impetus to make that switch?

John August: I'd done a little bit of fiction, of prose fiction, during that time. So, I'd done two short stories, which I enjoyed writing—just the chance to sort of break out of the screenplay form for a bit. But *Arlo Finch* was an idea that I'd had for a long time. I always wanted to do a story about my time in Boy Scouts, but sort of pushed into a magical place.

And it didn't quite feel like a movie. It didn't feel like a series. I didn't know sort of what it was going to be. I was in a conversation with this author about adapting his middle grade book and realized like, "Oh shit, I think the idea that I have is actually a middle grade book." And so that night I started writing it.

Had you read a lot of middle grade fiction at that point? Did you know what you were getting into?

John August: I was familiar with *Harry Potter*. I sort of knew what I had read at that age. So middle grade is really anything from a precocious 3rd grader up through 7th, 8th graders. I knew a general sense of what that was like and that the protagonist would be about that age. I had a sense of sort of what it was.

The voice of middle grade writing is actually about the voice of screenplays: it's the scene description and all that stuff. And that it should be about that same level of kind of easy readability. And so, it felt like it ended up being a pretty natural fit.

Was it an easy transition from the screenplay mindset to the novel mindset?

John August: Yes and no. I would say that in terms of arranging words on the page, once you get over the differences—which is how dialogue is handled, the sense of place and time—once you get over some of those things. In fact, you have more senses that you can describe: the temperature of the air, you can describe a lot of textures, smells and memories. You have that sort of that introspection that you don't have in screenplays. But once you get past those and get comfortable with that, it wasn't that different.

The biggest challenge for I think most screenwriters going into it is just the sheer amount of words you end up needing to generate in order to finish a book. And that my day's work would be like this many paragraphs, which got to be kind of frustrating at times.

I was talking to a playwright friend who writes plays all the time and they're produced everywhere and he's a great mystery playwright. And I said, "You should write a mystery novel." And he said, "Too many words, too many words."

John August: Yes, too many words. That really is, I think, the common lament.

So, having permission to write that much prose, which you weren't allowed to do before, how long did it take you to get that up to speed and be comfortable doing that?

John August: It was a pretty quick transition. I started the book on November 1st. So, I did it during a NaNoWriMo, which is the goal of like, you're cranking through 1500 or something words per day. And I wasn't hitting those targets, but I was definitely hitting targets where I was getting a lot of stuff written.

And once I had eight chapters written—and sort of a sense of what the rest of the book was—that's when I got a really good book agent and we set it up and we sold it as a trilogy to Macmillan.

I didn't have a good sense then of just how much work it was going to be to write those three books. And if I had known that, I probably would have made some different choices. Because it really ended up taking three years of my working life to get those done. I did some other stuff during that time, but there was always a book due. And that was a frustrating thing. And it's sort of hanging over you.

I know. Had I done better research, I'd know this: Is the podcast that you created about Arlo Finch and the creation of Arlo Finch still available?

John August: It is. *Launch* is still up anywhere you find podcasts.

Okay. Were there any other things that you instinctively knew as a screenwriter that you found helpful when it came to writing the books, like structuring things or dialogue?

John August: Yeah. I mean, screenplays are always about getting to the next thing. There's very much a sense of urgency and time in screenplays. And books have that ability to sort of veer off and explore and sort of paddle in the water for a long time. And I think I was more focused on the 'right now' of it all and getting things moving ahead because of that. I think that's a natural screenwriting instinct.

And I would also say there's a difference in scenes in books versus scenes in movies. Scenes in movies are very clear, like you're in a space, you're in a time. There's boundaries on things that just don't exist in the same way in books.

And finding that middle ground where it felt like this is a closed off moment—versus in a book, you can cover three years over the course of a paragraph. I didn't let myself do that, but there were cases where I did use sort of the powers of fiction to compress and expose things that would be very difficult to do in a movie or a series.

I tried to never think about the adaptation while writing the chapters. I tried to make sure that the book was the best version of the book. And that it was someone else's problem, how this is going to be adapted into a movie or series.

What about dialogue? Because I do both screenwriting and novel writing, I hear from novelists all the time saying, "Oh, you're so lucky with screenwriting, because you can write so much dialogue." And the fact is you can't, and there isn't that much dialogue in a movie compared to a book. What did

that feel like for you, having that freedom to suddenly let them talk a little more?

John August: Yeah, and also the ability—when and how you switch speakers. And how you make it clear to the audience what's really happening, just a block of dialogue, staying in one character's voice all the time, you're going to cut between the two of them.

And the way that 'he says' and 'she says' become invisible to the reader. That's all a strange thing to get used to as you're working in the form. And it's the boundaries of what is said and what is not said. They talked about this without having to actually sort of put in all the words there.

I enjoyed it, but I do think movie dialogue—play dialogue—is more accurate to the way the scene would actually happen, generally. There's a sense that books—especially because they're often written in this sort of past memory form—they are approximations of what would have actually happened.

You mentioned determining whose point of view something's from. And I seem to remember the first book is pretty much one point of view, but you do do a little head hopping after that. As a screenwriter you're writing, essentially, from the audience point of view. How did you determine— because you knew how to do the audience point of view really well—how did you determine when you sat down to write *Arlo* whose head you're going to be in at any given time?

John August: With *Arlo Finch*, what felt natural—which is actually true to sort of all middle grade fiction—is that it's a third person perspective, but very, very close to you. And so, you're sort of like just over his shoulder. And you tend to only know the things that that character knows. And that made a lot of sense. And the first book keeps strict POV that way.

In the second book, just because of events that happened, I did need to be able to cut to a different character's point of view. And so, it was really making clear that I was going to be elevating Indra to the ability to tell a story without Arlo being in the scene, by giving her a lot more agency and a lot more individual perspective early in the book. So that by the time it became her, most people don't notice that we're in a chapter without Arlo.

As you were going through this process and you're writing in this new fashion, what did you miss that you can do in a screenplay that you can't do in a novel, like music and things like that?

John August: Yeah, I mean, certainly a music cue. The ability to cut to a new thing and just to have a hard cut. You kind of can do it in a book, but it's not quite the same. You can do that sort of—like a sentence, two blank lines—and then you're in a new place and you're establishing a new space and time. But it's a little bit strange to do it. It's not as natural. And we see writers trying to do it too much. It's like they're trying to approximate the screenplay without getting into the slug lines. I missed that.

I missed the efficiency of it, the ability to sort of have incomplete sentences. The ability to just have three words, dash, dash, into some dialogue is a great, powerful, efficient way that we can do stuff in a screenplay that just doesn't work in a book. You have to end up finishing out those sentences.

One of the things that when I'm asked to talk about this— because I'm in the novel writing world now, but I was in the screenwriter world before and that's a nice hook, "Hey, let's have John talk about that"— is the ability that screenwriters

have (and novelists have, too, if they remember to do it) to surprise people To build in a surprise.

And one of the examples I always use—although I'm blanking on the character's name—but at the end of *Go,* there's a moment where they go, "Oh my god, we forgot character's name)!" And we as audience members had also forgotten. And it was very well laid in, that surprise. Can you think of any techniques that you've used in screenwriting like that, that helped you structure and create those sorts of moments in *Arlo*?

John August: Yeah, I think certainly the second Arlo Finch book, because it ultimately involves time travel, but we're sort of hiding the fact that it's gonna be time travel for quite a long period in it. Laying in those kind of the setups feels very natural in screenwriting, making sure that you're actually setting up and paying off those moments.

And sometimes as the writer, you know that you're doing it, you know what you're setting up. And other times you don't know what you're setting up. I think a lot of books are written kind of by the seat of their pants. And Arlo was kind of by the seat of my pants. But I definitely had a sense of where things were going. I would stop myself and just sort of outline out the rest of the book to make sure that everything would actually fit back together again at the end.

I think one of the differences you have to really encounter when working with a novel is that a person is going to see a movie all at once. They're going to sit down, they're going to give you, in theory, their entire attention for those two hours. With a book, they're giving you their full attention, which is great. But you don't know if they're going to put down a book for three days and then come back. Are they going to remember all those things? And so, I felt like I did need to sometimes do a little bit more handholding, to remind people about what had happened. Because I couldn't count on the fact that they remembered that detail from one hundred pages ago.

How do you tell the new reader what's come before without boring the old reader? How much thought did you put into that? I know you have some experience with television series and the concept of "Previously on ..." How did you approach that?

John August: I deliberately tried not to do that. And so, both the second and third book sort of start in the middle of the action. And then, as I needed to—if there was stuff I needed to call back from an earlier time—I would do it sort of right before you needed to remember that information. So, I wouldn't do it like, "Well, as we all know." But I would sort of say like, "In the time since, Arlo battled the hag..." Or whatever. I would fill that stuff in when it was appropriate.

I think one of the things that is nice about the novel form is that you do have a direct relationship with the reader. And so, you can just tell the reader things directly in ways that wouldn't work in a screenplay generally.

You mentioned that you sort of went by the seat of your pants when it came to the structuring of the stories. How often do you do that in your screenplay writing? How often do you not necessarily know 50 pages ahead?

John August: Pretty often. I know how it's going to end. I know what the emotional beats are that I need to hit. I'm often not sure quite how I'm going to do that while I'm doing it.

A thing that's important and different about writing the books versus writing a movie, is that I tend to write screenplays out of sequence. So, I'll write whatever scene appeals to me at the moment, because I know it's all going to fit back together at the end. It didn't feel possible with a book. I felt like I needed to sort of keep pushing forward with a book.

And deliberately, with the books, I would not—once I finished a chapter—I wouldn't go back and rewrite it or tweak it. I would just start working on the next chapter and always be moving forward.

And so, I think with screenplays—because I'm ping ponging all around in the script—I'm figuring out the whole thing kind of all at once. You know, if I'm writing that last sequence, I get a good sense of, "Oh, I need to set that up earlier on," and how it's all going to fit together.

It's interesting because Lee Goldberg says that he writes an outline, but he rewrites the outline as he's writing the book. And that the outline is done about a week before the book is done. You say that you just drive forward and go back and fix things. Which isn't really the way you do movie scripts. But you're in kind of a tighter frame there anyway with a film script. What is your rewrite process like and how is that different from your screenplay rewriting process?

John August: All three of the *Arlo Finch* books had very little rewriting. I mean, I would say 95 percent of what's in those books was within those chapters as I saved them the first time. I didn't go back and do a lot of wholesale rewriting of stuff. I really aimed for, "This feels like the chapter. This feels like the moment right from the start." There wasn't a lot of cutting. There wasn't a lot of, "Let me rethink how that all works."

In the second book, there were sometimes where, about midway through, I realized, "Okay, the time travel thing is not going to work if I don't make some changes earlier on to make some stuff fit." But, on the whole, it was very much the initial version was the final version.

And that's probably the thing I liked most about the *Arlo Finch* experience, is that those books are exactly the words I wanted there to be. My version is the final version, which in a movie situation never happens. With a movie, you're always making a plan for a thing that's going to change.

Do you think your ability to sit down and basically just write *Arlo Finch* from beginning to end was aided by the fact that you make your living writing stories and that you have—like you said—read all those screenplays? You have it built into your muscle memory as to when the story is going awry and how to fix that while the train is moving?

John August: I think a large part of the reason why I did the books in the first place is I kind of wondered if I could. I wanted to challenge myself and it was nice feeling like a beginner again. It was nice feeling like a person who wasn't an expert in something. Because while I enjoyed writing screenplays, I've gotten a little bit bored. And I found myself sometimes making dangerous choices and setting impossible deadlines. Or pursuing projects that really weren't necessarily the thing I should be writing, just because they were exciting and challenging for me because they scared me a bit.

And so, it was nice in this case to just have a whole kind of writing that I wasn't quite sure I could do. Part of the reason why I did *The Launch* podcast was to document the experience of learning this whole new thing and learning this whole new structure.

A similar thing happened when I did the Broadway musical version of *Big Fish*. I had to learn a completely different set of vocabulary and ways of working to make that happen.

So, was there one thing that as a screenwriter—as a person with screenwriting skills—that you think was an advantage

for you when you sat down to do something new like writing a novel?

John August: I definitely have a very clear visual sense. And so, as you read *Arlo Finch*—and the people who read and liked it— you really can see it. You can really see and feel and get a sense of the places that you're at. It's like you're watching the movie as you're in it. And I think that was a goal. And that was just also something I'm very used to being able to do from screen-writing.

And I don't know—if I weren't a screenwriter and I was just approaching the novel from scratch—I might have been more stuck in characters' heads. I might've been dwelling too long on interior motivation. I think because everything in screenplays has to be externalized, I was definitely mindful of externalizing those things.

At the same time, Arlo is a kind of passive internal character, and it was part of the joy of writing to break away from the sense of protagonism and the sense of like, "Oh, this has to be the disruptor who's going to change everything." I really wanted to have the wallflower hero. And it was fun to be able to think of it that way.

Now, as I remember, when the first book was finished, you went out and did live events with your readers, with kids. What did you learn? I mean, screenwriters never get to go meet their audience. What was that like?

John August: The whole routine of school visits is crazy. And it's sort of an under-documented aspect of putting out a middle grade book is that you're expected to tour all these schools. It's fun at the start. And then it becomes just like, "Oh my God, I'm a person who gives the same presentation a hundred times."

I probably did it forty times. And you're making the same jokes and the same routine. And it really just burns a hole in you. And I don't know that I would do it again. I'm doing a graphic novel right now, which is again, it's sort of a new interesting challenge. But when that comes out, I'm not sure I'm going to do the school visits. Because as I talked to more middle grade authors, once upon a time it really was the way that you sold books. And it's not clear now that it really moves the needle at all.

But it is sort of fun to get in front of your readers.

John August: A hundred percent. It really is. And it's been great. Yes, I have folks who love my movies, which is great and they want me to sign things. But when the kids really love the *Arlo Finch* books, that is special.

So, for aspiring novelists, is there one piece of advice you'd give them, based on your experience as a screenwriter who went on to write novels?

John August: I think it's hitting your word counts, which seems so tough. But during the time I was writing the second *Arlo Finch* book, I started running and started running longer races. Ultimately, you can get the shoes, you can get all the gear, but ultimately what you need to do is just keep doing miles. And that's what ultimately gets you there.

Frankenweenie was three weeks of work to make that. You can just zoom through a script. And there's just no way to zoom through a book. A book is just going to be a slog. And you're going to feel trapped in the middle of it at some point. That's just how it goes.

Yes, but you've had that experience as a screenwriter of being on the clock because you're being paid to get something done in a certain amount of time. And I imagine that

creates a discipline that's just sort of built in. You said it was three years of this book hanging over you each time. But you have that same experience with a script hanging over you, don't you?

John August: Yeah, but I think it's different. I mean, scripts—when worse comes to worse—I really could buckle down and sprint and sort of finish the thing. Even if that meant writing 50 pages in a week. You can do that.

You can't sprint through a book. It's just not possible. It's just going to be a slog. And it reminded me a little bit of the one TV show that I was show running. There's just always that crushing like, "Oh shit." There's this thing that's always going to be hanging over you. It's like your entire life is doing this thing.

KELLYE GARRETT

Kellye Garrett began her writing career as a journalist, working as an editorial assistant at <u>The New York Daily News</u> and then an assistant editor at <u>Vibe</u> magazine in the early 2000s. However, she found herself wanting to create her own stories rather than just report on others'.

This led Garrett to pursue a Master's degree in screenwriting from USC's prestigious film school, where she was one of only 25 students in her class handpicked by the program's dean. After graduating in 2005, Garrett broke into television writing with a staff job on the CBS procedural <u>Cold Case</u>.

When her screenwriting career stalled in her early 30s, Garrett decided to finally pursue the novel writing she had long wanted to tackle but been intimidated by. Drawing from her background in mysteries and procedurals, she crafted the acclaimed Detective by Day mystery series starter <u>Hollywood Homicide</u>, which went on to win numerous top awards like the Agatha, Anthony and Lefty for Best First Novel.

A key insight Garrett offers is the importance of creating compelling chapter cliffhangers to keep readers hooked, something she learned from writing act breaks for television shows. As she states: "I want every chapter to end on a high point. I hope the reader says, 'Oh, I just have to stay up and read one more chapter and find out.'"

Was writing always a path you wanted to take?

Kellye Garrett: Yes. Since I was like five.

Why was that? How did that manifest?

Kellye Garrett: I don't know. I mean, you're five, you just know. So, I guess some people want to be like firefighters. I wanted to be a writer. I think it helped that my mother was a really big reader. I think my aunt said when she moved out of my family's house when I was graduating college, she had a thousand books that she took with her. She packed and took with her. She did not purge them or give them away. She took them with her.

So, I think books have always had a special place in my heart. I just knew. I mean, did that make it easier? No, I still struggle with it. But I knew. I was afraid—I think one of the reasons why I did screenwriting—was because I was afraid to write books.

Okay. Why were you afraid of books?

Kellye Garrett: A fear of failure, fear of success. Like the dream: people talk about dreams a lot, but sometimes it's scary to pursue them.

So, I know you went to USC. How did that happen? What were you doing before USC? And why did you pick USC?

Kellye Garrett: My first job out of college was an editorial assistant for the features department at *The New York Daily News*. Lasted a year. Hated it, literally hated it, hated it every day. I think part of it was, it was my first job out of school. So, I think there's that struggle. And the other part was just, it was not a great place to work.

And then I got a job as an assistant editor at *Vibe*. And at that time, *Vibe* magazine was—I can't say what it is now—but in the early 2000s, *Vibe* was huge. If you were a black person, a young black person who wanted to be in magazine journalism, you wanted to work at *Vibe*. So, I was very lucky that I got an Assistant Editor job at *Vibe*.

I was working on what they call the front of the book section. And I wasn't covering music. I was covering film and TV. And, you know, journalism is great, but you're really reporting what other people are doing. And so, I was like, okay, I can either report on all these people doing really great TV and film. Or I could do it myself.

And so I applied to film school. I applied to USC, UCLA, and I think Syracuse. And Howard Rodman (Dean of USC) called me to tell me I got in. So, I knew pretty early I got USC. I did not get UCLA. I did get Syracuse. And USC is USC, right? So, I'm still paying off my student loans for USC. And it's been like 20 plus years. I graduated in 2005. I'm still paying my student loans off.

So, it was a very expensive venture, but, you know, it's such a competitive industry. And I don't think you need to go to school for (screenwriting), but I think USC is—it's such an incestuous industry, where it's who you know, and names and things like that. But as nepotism, it helped having that on my resume, right? To say, not only am I an aspiring TV writer, I'm an aspiring TV writer who went to the top film school. Only 25 students were in my class. It was grad school. So, to say I was one of 25 at USC and I got called personally by the Dean, I think that helped.

I lasted, I think, maybe like two or three years. And once again, one thing about me, John, I'm gonna leave if I'm not happy. And so, I lasted maybe four years and I was, "You know what? No."

Enough was enough?

Kellye Garrett: Enough was enough.

Do you remember, was there like a light bulb moment during that grad school program where something just clicked? You went, "Oh, I get how this works," when it came to writing and creating a TV or movie story?

Kellye Garrett: I think I can still break down. If you gave me a movie, I could probably still break it down into a sequence structure. I haven't even thought about that in probably fifteen years, but I can still be, "Oh, here's the point of attack. Here's the end of the act. Here's the midpoint. Here's the end of the third act." I could break down any movie still.

I think it was great in terms of showing you the basics and the stuff that you could probably get in books. There are certain things that I learned that I think that, like you said, helped me. Still help me to this day in book writing. Is it worth it, whatever, like thousands of dollars of debt I'm still in? Maybe, maybe not. But it was helpful.

You left USC and was your first job as a writing assistant? Is that the first thing you did?

Kellye Garrett: Yes, I was a writer's PA for a show called *Angela's Eyes,* which was on Lifetime. And so, it's cool. I wasn't in the writer's room, but I was in the writer's office. I was answering the phone and getting lunch, but it was kind of cool to see that process.

And then I was lucky where my friend and I became writing partners and we got into an NBC writing program—I don't even know if it's still around. Maybe it's called Writers on the Verge. So, we got into this writing program from NBC, which is meant to feed people into the industry. So again, another thing for your resume to show, "Oh, I'm not just any TV writer, aspiring TV writer."

And then we got on the show *Cold Case*. And then my writing partner and I broke up and then we got let go from the show. So, it was very quick. Very up and down.

Well, that's a writer's path. So, you and your partner are working at least briefly on *Cold Case*. Was that a room situation, were you—?

Kellye Garrett: It was a room, and it was interesting. A writer's room is essentially a conference room: people all sit around and talk about whatever that episode is. And it's great. Because it's just really creative. You're throwing out ideas and stuff.

On the other hand, it sucked though. Because most jobs, you don't really work eight hours a day, right? You might have a meeting and then you might be taking a break, and you can kind of let your brain breathe, right?

A writers' room, you're in that room. It's you and like ten other people. And you can't go off. You have to be paying attention. So, I would leave work and I would be so mentally exhausted. And I would just go home and be quiet.

I think also it was kind of this pressure. My writing partner and I, we weren't getting along that great. And there was kind of a pressure of TV, because they spend millions of dollars per episode. So, they're not going to let you—the studios and networks—are not going to let you do whatever you want. So, it's a lot of hands in the pot, I guess, I don't even know what the phrase is.

So, you would have the idea for the show. For us, we did Japanese internment camps. And that's all we knew. And then we spent a week in the room, breaking it down. And we went and we had to do an outline that had to get approved by the showrunner, had to get approved by the network, had to get approved by the studio. Then we wrote the episode and the same thing: it had to get approved by the show runner, had to get approved by the network, had to get approved by the studio.

That is just such a process that I don't miss it. I think by the time everyone's done with their feedback, what you wrote might not be anything what you wanted to write, what you thought it was going to be. Sometimes it's better. Sometimes it's worse.

The funny thing is, even when you see a bad TV show—same thing with books—I can't knock a bad book or a bad TV show. Because I know a lot of people spent hours upon hours working on this. And so, it was bad, but they still put their heart and soul into that. So, I have to give them props for that.

What did you learn about getting notes and taking notes and processing notes during that process that you went on to use in novel writing?

Kellye Garrett: I think I am not naive enough to think that I am perfect, right? I've had issues where I did not get notes from an editor and I was, "I know this isn't good. I want this to be the best it can be." And I know that sometimes I'm—most of the time—it's going to be a collaboration process.

I think I got—maybe my editor might think differently—I got good at looking at notes and saying, "This might not necessarily be the solution, but they are pointing out a problem." So, I think that helped me a lot.

On the flip side—because of what I said earlier, with having so many people in the pot—I do think I am really strong now with being, "This is my book. I wrote every word in this book." And if my editor has notes for me, and I've tried them and they did not work. And I do feel confident enough to be, "Look, I tried it, it did not work." Or, "No, I'm not going to do that for XYZ."

I'm never rude about it. But I am very much—because of my having so many people and not thinking anything was mine before in TV writing—my book is mine. And I am the ultimate decider. Whereas with TV—and also especially movies—the writer is not the ultimate decider of what's going to be on screen.

That's a common theme I'm picking up from talking to you folks, is the surprise that a writer who has written for TV and movies has when they get notes on their book. And the editor says, "Use whatever you like. You don't like them. Don't use them." It's like, "Really? I don't have to do that?"

So, all right, you unfortunately get a good job right before a strike and you're out on the street again. You've always wanted to be a writer. You've been intimidated by books. How did *Hollywood Homicide* come about?

Kellye Garrett: I'm broke. No job.

My writing partner and I had broken up. I was writing spec scripts. And my agent at the time did not like any of them. And I was dead broke.

I think at the time I was doing a report writing for a PI (Private Investigator) firm. Hated that. They were interesting people. And it wasn't even sexy PI. It was, there was a slip out at a grocery store warehouse, that type of PI. I had to take the interview that the investigator did and make it into an interesting narrative of what happened.

And so, I was broke. I was probably in my early thirties. I don't want to do TV anymore. And I don't want to do this PI thing, this PI writing thing. What am I going to do with my life? And I was driving down the street. And in California they had billboards offering rewards for information about crimes.

And I saw one, offering a $10,000 or $15,000 reward for information on a murder. And literally my first thought was, "I should try to solve that. To get the reward money. I need money." And my mother would have killed me. It was a horrible idea for a human, like a real human being.

But then the second thought was, "Oh, that's a really good book idea." And so, it was at my lowest point. I had nothing to lose at that time. So, I'm, "Finally, I have a really good idea. Finally." I have these skills that I have learned. I feel very confident as a writer having worked as a journalist, having a master's degree, two writing degrees. (I think I've had three, my technical writing degree, too.) I have these degrees. I have these skills. I have this background. That's where it came from.

Initially, it was not about an actress or Hollywood. But my friend said, "Make her an actress." And I think anyone who reads *Hollywood Homicide*, it's so funny. I started it in 2011, even though it came out 2017. And you read it. And Dana (the main character) is so ambivalent about Hollywood in the book. And that's because that's how I felt. I joke: I was a semi-successful mega broke black writer. I can't make her exactly like me. So, she's a semi-famous mega broke black actress. So, a lot of the ambivalence that she has about Hollywood was how I felt at the time.

It's funny because with *Hollywood Ending*, I was in a completely different place in my life. And I didn't feel like that at all. So, it was kind of weird to have to kind of go back to that. But it was therapeutic in a way.

So, you have—at the point of starting that novel—you have a lot of varied kinds of writing experience. You have degrees and you've broken stories and written stories. What was your level of confidence going in? And what had you learned in the past that made it easier for you to tackle that first novel?

Kellye Garrett: I'm still not confident about it. But I think there are certain things I've learned about stories and having worked in procedurals about how to craft mysteries and how to craft twists and how to plant things that I think really helped me.

I think to this day, people are like, "Oh, your books are very fast paced. Your books have good dialogue, your books feel cinematic." And I think it's because of my background.

There's bad things too. I'm really bad at description, still to this day. So, I think there's good and bad with it.

I just felt the combination—of it being such a low point in my life and having nothing to lose—I think that honestly helped me more than, "Oh, I can finally prepare to write a book." It's more like, "I'm finally no longer afraid to write a book."

You know, the whole describing thing, it's come up several times. And it's an issue I have as well, because my background is in screenwriting. When we're writing a screenplay or a TV piece, we're writing to describe it enough so that the department heads know what to do, or that the executive knows what we're talking about. And they fill in all that stuff. Was it a major mountain for you to climb to take on the roles of all those heads of departments as you're writing the book?

Kellye Garrett: I'm gonna say no, just because I didn't do it. You know, it's funny. I think my first drafts, I think, are good plot wise. I think for me, they're more about figuring out the plot. But then I have to go back in the second draft and put in emotion and character development. I had the ideas for the characters, but I gotta put it on the page.

I still don't—honestly though—if I read a book, I don't like reading descriptions. I don't know about you, but I'm, "Uh, the whole page about the room." I think that my mother is the same way. And she was joking, "I like reading your books, because I don't have to worry about a lot of description."

So, I still don't do a lot of it, but I try to do enough where you're like, "Oh, I have a somewhat idea, they're in a house and, you know, they're in the living room and this and that." But I'm not going to go on for two pages about the tree or something.

I'm amazed when people do that. I don't care. What's the next thing that happens? What's the next thing that happens? Which brings me to our next question. You talked about pace and in TV—particularly in procedurals—pace is important. How did knowing how to do that and create compelling act outs help you create chapter cliffhangers that keep people reading?

Kellye Garrett: I made a point to have the act out, which you know, but I'll still describe it. It's that last scene before the commercial break. They want you to sit through the commercials—commercials for toothpaste you're going to buy anyway —to sit there to find out what happened, not change the channel. And so, I want every chapter to end on a high point. I hope the reader says, "Oh, I just have to stay up and read one more chapter and find out." That's—to me—the ultimate compliment, saying, "I stayed up too late reading a book."

So, I think that really helped me. In TV, you have a set period of time—I don't know, I don't really watch as much TV as I used to, so I don't know what it is. But it used to be forty-two minutes for an hour show. And so, you literally have to use every moment to move the plot along. And so, I think that helped me too: every scene has something that moves the plot. Whether it's an actual setting up, introducing a new character, or maybe planting something that pays off later. Or doing a bigger plot reveal.

But to me—because that's what I had to do in TV writing—every scene in my books, there's something plot-wise or book-wise or story-wise that's going to move that story along. Again, it's not going to be just this woman walking down the street, literally smelling the roses. If she's smelling the roses, it's because it's going to come back later. And it's like, that's how the person died.

I also believe in having an A story, B story, even C story, even if it doesn't fit or move the A story, the mystery along. In *Like a Sister*, there is this whole relationship with her father, which to me is the heart of the story: having them come together, having her dealing with her daddy issues. With *Missing White Woman*, she has unresolved issues with an estranged best friend who comes back in her life to help her. So, I think not every scene has to fit the main story, but it needs to kind of move some part of the story along.

Are you breaking the stories the same way you did in TV?

Kellye Garrett: Oh my gosh, it's changed. It used to be for the first two—I've had four books—the first two books, I did really long outlines. And the end of act—this is the end of act twist—and this and that. And I've kind of evolved as I have been writing more. I don't know if it's confidence or familiarity. I don't know what it is. But when I first started, I very much held on to that outline. It was like a safety blanket. I hate writing. I hate the blank page,

But you're going into a novel with a pretty structured idea of beginning, middle and who did it. Are you making it up as you go?

Kellye Garrett: No, I always knew who did it. And I still have the basic beats.

How willing are you to deviate once you get going?

Kellye Garrett: Oh my God, even with the first two books, I would write like probably a 30-page outline. And every time I get to the third act, I'd throw it away. Because when I was writing, I'm like, "Oh, now that I'm writing and I know these characters, this isn't what happened." So, I'm not afraid to deviate from it. I think of it as a safety blanket that sometimes I can just throw off.

Pretend you're talking to someone who's either just written their first novel or about to write their first novel. You have this background in TV writing, you have degrees from USC, you've written for TV and novels. Is there one piece of advice you'd give them from your experience in screenwriting that you think would help a beginning novelist?

Kellye Garrett: I would say every scene has to move the story forward. That's what I used to tell my mentees in Pitch Wars.

What is Pitch Wars?

Kellye Garrett: Pitch Wars was—at the time—it was the biggest online mentoring program for writers. I got my agent through it.

So, what they do is they would take an emerging unagented writer, pair them with a writer who is a little farther along—like either they have a book, or they have at least an agent. And they would spend about two to three months revising the book. And then they'd have what they call an agent showcase, where we would show the first 250 words and a brief synopsis. And agents would come and look at it and request a copy. I met my agent through Pitch Wars. I had five mentees and most of my mentees have book deals now. So, it's kind of cool.

We closed it a couple of years ago. But for a good, probably ten years, it was a really great place for emerging writers to get help. Almost like a mini grad school program.

Was there anything that you learned which you might have been surprised to learn when you were mentoring? Because often, as a teacher, you do learn things from the students. Was there anything you walked away with from that experience?

Kellye Garrett: I mean, it's just amazing. Talent is talent. And there are just some people who have really amazing writing talent. I was blessed that all my mentees did. And sometimes— and I'm not going to say it's for any of them—but sometimes you just need to learn how to write. Learn the best way to write the book.

I think, again, for mysteries—like I said—it's planting clues, paying off, having the story move along. And having these good kind of twists that happen at the end of every act, so it takes the story in a new direction. And I hope that my mentees learned that and they're taking that with them. I used to make them all outline. I don't think any of them outline anymore, but I used to make them all outline. Just to get an understanding of that process.

How do you think your TV writing experience and your graduate school experience helped shape you as a novelist?

Kellye Garrett: I think it was a shortcut in terms of learning structure and thinking as a writer—a mystery writer—in terms of plot and twists and characters and having a good high concept. I think it helped in those ways.

I think having worked in the industry—because it's such a creative field—people don't realize it's a business, right? And it's very much a business. But it's not even like a business where, "I'm like a lawyer and I know if I start at this law firm and I work 100 hours a week that I can possibly be partner in ten years." It's not even that type of business.

It's a business that makes no sense. And so, I didn't come in with rose colored glasses. I didn't come in thinking I was going to be the next Stephen King (and I'm not), so it helped in that way. I think it helped me in how I view the industry. Some might say I'm too cynical about it, but I think it helped.

I have worked in Hollywood, which is the ultimate creative business that attracts the most, I will say colorful personalities, even though I want to say other words. It helped me come into this business where my expectations are very low.

Every book's a blessing. I might never write again.

NICK MOHAMMED

Nick Mohammed is a versatile British actor, comedian and writer who has made his mark across TV, film, radio and stage. He first gained widespread acclaim for his enduring character, Mr. Swallow, who he has portrayed in various shows over the past decade.

However, his talents extend far beyond that beloved comedic persona. He is the creator of the Sky One series <u>Intelligence</u> and has written for radio shows like his own <u>Nick Mohammed in Bits</u>. His acting credits span guest roles on hits like <u>Miranda</u>, <u>Life's Too Short</u> and <u>Drifters</u>, as well as voicing Piglet in the 2018 film <u>Christopher Robin</u>.

Mohammed's biggest breakout role came in 2020 when he was cast as the Kit Manager turned coach Nathan "Nate" Shelley, on the widely acclaimed Apple TV+ comedy, <u>Ted Lasso</u>.

Beyond his on-screen work, he's also published two novels - <u>The Young Magicians</u> and <u>The Vanishing Trick</u>—a middle-grade fiction series drawing from his own childhood passion for magic and sleight of hand.

His background in television writing helped provide the discipline and structural skills needed to craft an engaging, propulsive narrative, while still allowing his creative passions to shine through.

NOTE: This interview was recorded for my podcast, "Behind the Page: The Eli Marks Podcast," where I talk to magicians about the art and craft of magic.

One of the major reasons I wanted to have you on the show was because of this book series—it's a two-book series at this point—*The Young Magicians* series, which is terrific. Where did the idea come from?

Nick Mohammed: Well, it was a quite an organic thing, really. You know, I'd never set out to write prose even, not children's fiction or anything. I was doing a Mr. Swallow show, his retelling of *Dracula*, actually.

And one of the editors or publishers at Penguin Random House happened to be in the audience, not because my agent had sent them or anything like that. And they left their card afterwards and said, "Oh, it'd be great to, you know, I feel like you've got quite a silly sense of humor off the back of that show. Have you ever considered writing for children?" And I said, "No, but you know, I'm up for chatting about it." And so, we subsequently met after The Fringe.

I just sort of did a page outline on a few ideas. I thought, "Oh, that might be a fun thing, you know, for children's fiction." But the one that really sparked their interest—and I guess that I had the most sort of connection to and authenticity to, because of my upbringing within magic and loving magic as a kid—they were like, "Oh, that's the idea."

And I was a huge fan of all those shows, like *The Goonies* and things like that. The idea of these slightly geeky, gawky characters, sort of outsider characters, who come together and solve these crimes or uncover these plots or something. But use their magic—sleight of hand and abilities—to help. That felt like a really fun area.

I mean, look, it took me <u>ages</u> to write. I was acting at the time. Finn was born and maybe even Arthur as well during the lifetime of me writing that. It took a good couple of years. But I'm so proud; everything else I've done (whether it be telly or film or something, or even script writing), it's so rare to write a thing that you can hold. Something that you can hold, this tangible thing. And it'll never change; I can't change it. It's there, it exists on a bookshelf and in libraries. And I can see it. And I love it. I love that.

Don't get me wrong, it was a real challenge, and it took a while. But, yeah, I loved it. Who knows when I'll have time to write some more, but I'd love to at some point. But I really enjoyed— particularly that first one—it really was so cathartic. Just getting to write about—even the way the Magic Circle's presented, obviously so much of it is tongue in cheek—but I was able to pour so much of my childhood into it: So much of what I found funny growing up and going to conventions and my experience of magic and so on.

It sort of does poke fun at magic here and there, but I really enjoyed doing it.

I've talked to a lot of TV writers and screenwriters who've gone on to write novels, and I'm always curious: how did your work—as a screenwriter and a sketch writer and writing episodic television—how did that inform your writing of the novel? How did it help? What leg up did it give you that a normal novelist might not have?

Nick Mohammed: Well, I don't know if it did help. It's so diffi-cult to know the answer to that. Because I guess I knew I could write funny stuff. I knew I could write funny dialogue, I guess, because I'd done that before.

But I didn't know if I could world build in the way that you need to in a work of prose. And I didn't necessarily know how to tell a really good story that felt like I want the reader to feel: excited at the end of a chapter and want to know what's happening. I didn't necessarily know how to do that. I mean, I knew what books I liked and liked as a child. And I reread a lot of stuff and tried to get my head around it.

But I remember even Penguin saying, "Just have a go at it. And then, once there's something there—when we know whether it's in the right direction—there's support here. You can have a story editor, copy editor, we can work on stuff together."

So, I kind of wrote quite blindly in a way. I worked on the story first and got that signed off in the first instance. And worked out what each chapter was going to be. And also—crucially—how the magic tricks were going to be done. So that I knew what you could hint at and seed along the way before revealing it at the end.

But other than that, I was just like, "Well, here we go, start writ-ing." And, you know, some days it was like, great, it's flowing and I feel good. And other days it's like, I feel like I'm writing and I'm just going to delete all this, because I just don't know what it is, and it's just probably filler and it's not advancing the story.

It was—overwhelmingly for the most part—a really fun and fulfilling process, albeit it took a while.

It sounds like—even though you don't think so—that your

TV writing experience helped. I'm thinking in particular, did *Intelligence* come later?

Nick Mohammed: *Intelligence*. Okay. It did come out. Yes. It did come later. I would have been working on the pilot. Though I probably would have been pitching stuff in that world.

In that instance (on *Intelligence*), I'm sure you had an outline of where the series was going to go. And you had to work out all the beats. And so you had a very solid outline to write that series. And you sat down to do the same thing with the book. You weren't a discovery writer. You were a writer who went, "Oh, I know that I need to have the beats figured out." And you'd learn that from TV writing.

Nick Mohammed: Yes, definitely. Yes, I guess you're right. I think that there's a discipline in breaking it down into smaller achievable chunks. Which is useful to do in both telly/film writing and crossing over into book writing. The outline stages, treatments, character development, series arcs, or narrative arc, whatever. Yeah, I guess knowing my way around that definitely will have helped.

I still found it daunting—the idea of a book—because a book feels like proper. It feels like it's a <u>book</u>, you know, it's got a beginning and a middle and an end. And once it's there, there's no way out. You know, it just felt quite proper.

I think I thought at the time, I was like, "Oh, I wonder if this will be the start of something quite big for me. Will I suddenly find myself being a children's author?" And actually, I didn't. There was a bit of a splash at the start. Then it just became, "Okay, well, when's the next book?" kind of thing. And, you know, it's sort of, you're onto the next one and you're onto the next one.

And it was happening at a time when I was then getting very busy as a TV writer and as an actor as well. So, it naturally started to take the back foot a little bit.

But then interestingly—I guess slightly off the back of *Ted Lasso* and people becoming a bit more familiar with me and my work —there is actual interest in developing it for telly. And it's quite nice to go back into the book and be like, "Ah, now how will I adapt this for telly?" Rather than my experience as a TV writer going into prose. Now I can take something and start thinking about it for telly. So, you know, that's quite fun.

Before we leave *The Young Magicians* series, do you have any advice for someone who's starting a novel? Something you learned that maybe you got from screenwriting and TV writing that helped you on that process?

Nick Mohammed: I think it's that idea of writing about something that you love, or something that you care about, or a story that you really want to tell. I think you really have to want to, because it's quite a thankless task. Especially in the first stages of writing something, because you don't have much to show for it. It obviously naturally grows, but it takes time. It certainly takes time from an idea into a book that you can hold, right?

So, I feel like it being something that you care about really helps with the day to day of, "Hey, I'm going to write about this thing," and it's actually something that really excites me or it's something that's important or that needs saying. That helps with the drive of it. But—like what we were saying before— being able to split it up into something that just feels a bit more manageable and doesn't feel as daunting is always really useful.

So that's where giving yourself the time to properly work up an outline, so that you feel like you've got almost like a blueprint to navigate your way through the writing process.

And setting deadlines, whether they're realistic or otherwise. I definitely missed tons of deadlines in writing it. They were more for my benefit to try and just get something done. But giving yourself a deadline is always a surefire way of at least trying to achieve sort of something within a time frame. And then if you need to extend it or something, well, then that's fine, that's on you.

So, I think just sort of making it manageable, but knowing that there are lots of books in the world, you know? As much as it can feel like a bit of a hurdle—or lots of hurdles—and there are lots of psychological barriers to calling yourself a writer and sitting down and writing and saying, "No, that's what I am doing. I'm a writer and I'm writing something and I'm an author." A lot of people do manage it and do it. So, knowing that it is within your grasp. And a lot of those people will have gone through exactly the same thing that you're feeling right now. So, you can grasp onto that a little bit.

That's excellent advice. I want to jump back to you mentioning creating an outline, whether it's for a series or for the book. I don't know if this is apocryphal. I don't know where I heard that Jason (Sudeikis) came up to you while shooting Episode Two or Three of Season One (of *Ted Lasso*), and said, "By the way, Nick, this is where Nate's going over the three seasons." Is that true?

Nick Mohammed: That's so true. That's 100% true.

That's phenomenal. When you look at a TV show like *Lost*, where it comes out that they're actually making it up as they went along. That (the *Ted Lasso* writers) had that foresight for that character is great. How did that help you?

Nick Mohammed: Not just me. I think a few characters knew where there were certain turning points in their story.

I felt so lucky. And I distinctly remember it: it's the gala episode in Season One, which is, I think, Episode Three or Four. And I remember it because Ted takes Nate as his date. So, Jason and I just had a lot of time just being next to each other during shooting, during set up, sitting next to each other at the table and stuff.

And I remember specifically him saying, "Just so you know, this is where...." I didn't know the level of detail and exactly at what point everything, but he says, "You're going to get promoted by the end of Season One. It's going to go to your head in Season Two. And it's *Empire Strikes Back*: basically you're going to turn on your master and you're going to then go to the dark side by the end of Season Two. And you're going to join West Ham, the rival club where Rupert is going to be at. And then Season Three is not so much a redemption story, but it's about forgiveness and acceptance. It follows a redemptive arc, but it's more about forgiveness than redemption."

But he outlined that as broadly as I have outlined that to you now, to me then. Because there's a very key point in that episode: Rupert has shown up and he takes the mic and at the end of that, everyone gets up and starts dancing. And Nate is sat back watching. And we made a very, very deliberate decision as to the reason. The viewer is meant to think, "Oh, Nate sat back, not joining in with this dancing because he's introverted, and he wouldn't be able to."

And that is true. There's an element that is true to the character at that point in his journey. But it's also true—and the way that I played it, even though it's in a wide shot and what Jason was very keen to get—was the idea of him sitting back and seeing that someone like Rupert has come in with all this power and has just changed the room. And look at what he's managed to achieve.

And that's going into the back of Nate's head, being like, "Hmm, oh, okay, okay. There's something to aspire to here." And him just taking it in. And in the end, it turns out obviously that he doesn't handle this new responsibility or this new power when he gets promoted very well at all. And it quickly spirals.

But the writers wanted to plant those seeds along the way. And they absolutely did. And they really paid dividends.

TOM STRAW

Tom Straw is a true renaissance man of mystery writing. He first made his mark as the anonymous ghostwriter behind the blockbuster Nikki Heat series, published under the name of fictional author Richard Castle from the hit TV show Castle. Those seven bestselling crime novels, written over the course of the show's eight-year run from 2009-2016, allowed Straw to keep his identity cleverly concealed, adding to the overall "Castle myth."

But Straw was far from a novice when he took on that ghostwriting assignment. He's an accomplished screenwriter and producer in his own right, earning Emmy and Writers Guild of America nominations for his work on hit shows like Night Court, Parker Lewis Can't Lose, Dave's World, Grace Under Fire, Cosby, Whoopi, and Nurse Jackie. His first published novel under his own name was 2007's The Trigger Episode, a mystery about a former combat photographer turned paparazzo.

After the successful Nikki Heat series, Straw returned to publishing fiction as himself with 2022's Buzz Killer. A member of the prestigious Mystery Writers of America, he continues crafting suspenseful tales from his home base in Connecticut. Straw's extensive TV writing background, with its emphasis on structure and meeting deadlines, has served him well as a novelist adept at crafting tightly plotted, page-turning mysteries.

Was being a writer always a goal, even as a kid?

Tom Straw: Yes. Absolutely. I promise I won't give you one-word answers. You know, it's funny, I probably didn't know it consciously, but I've always been attracted to the idea of telling stories in one form or another.

I can remember—you have to be of a certain age to remember these toys—but I can remember when I was in the single digit years, I got one of those typewriters that you twist the dial, and you punch, and you make one letter at a time. And I set out to write my neighborhood newspaper one day. I got halfway through one page and quit because it was a little tedious to do that. But as I look back on it, I can remember that little kid wanting to get stuff down on paper and sometimes in the ether.

Because eventually I ended up going to radio. I mean, that was really my first work, my first career, if you will. And that's a form of storytelling. You do it when you're a top 40-disc jockey or an album rock jock. You tend to do it in 30 second clips or 15 second clips, but you're constantly coming up with, "Okay, what am I going to say? How am I going to embellish?"

Exactly. You know, I've spoken a couple of times to Ken Levine—

Tom Straw: A dear friend of mine, a dear, dear friend.

—and I don't think he was on microphone when he mentioned this, but in addition to being a TV writer and a playwright and a radio guy, he's also a play-by-play announcer. And that same muscle is being used trying to engage an audience between things as a play-by-play

announcer that you probably had to deal with all the time as a disc jockey.

Tom Straw: There's no doubt about it. Ken and I go way back. We probably don't want to go too deeply into that, but I met him when I was in high school.

He was at UCLA and I was in high school. I started a radio station at my high school and then I was running for junior class president. And I, rather magnanimously, took myself off the air (when I say the air, I meant the speakers in the lunch court). And we needed to have somebody fill in for me on my Tuesday show.

And somebody knew this guy at UCLA named Ken Levine. And that's when we met. And he and I've been friends that long. He mentored me into television. He gave me my first two jobs in TV. We're still dear friends. He's a lifelong friend and always will be.

But you know, to go to your thing about sports: when I was in Seattle working at a radio station there, we carried the Mariners. And one of our talk show hosts was the official scorer and he wrote the baseball column for the local newspaper, *Seattle Times*. And his name was J. Michael Kenyon. I don't even know if he's still with us these days.

But I said to him one day, "How do you write about a baseball game every night?" And he said, "It's this difficult, but it's also this simple: Every game has a story. And my job is to figure out what the story of the game is and then write a column that supports it and highlights it. Sometimes it's about errors, sometimes it's about arguments, sometimes it's about nothing happening."

But that was very enlightening for me as a storyteller to recognize that even in something that appears to be pedestrian—I won't say baseball's pedestrian, but certainly quotidian, day to day—you can still look at something and say, "Well, what's new about this? What is it telling me? And what can I then tell a reader?"

That's got to be a hugely helpful skill when you then get into TV writing—we're jumping ahead here—where you've got, at the time you were starting, probably twenty-two episodes a year that they were trying to do.

Tom Straw: Sometimes twenty-four.

Yes. How do you take these same five characters, whatever it is, and come up with something new for them to do for twenty-two minutes? That still leaves them sort of the same.

Tom Straw: Oh, I can answer that. And that is if you're on a show where the characters are very well defined and have life in them. And then are in an ensemble that plays off the aspects of the other characters' characters, in a situation that makes great sense. You know, those things are hard to come by. I mean, you know, we talk about Ken Levine. You talk about *MASH*, talk about *Cheers*, you know, you talk about shows that could still be going if they wanted to. And that's really where you find the gold.

I can remember I was on a show called *Parker Lewis Can't Lose*. It was on Fox, and it was a high school show. A very fun show to write. It was one of those shows that we came up with all sorts of stories.

But I remember very well exhausted at the end of the season, having done twenty-two episodes of that show, longing for the hiatus break when I could just kind of like read something that didn't have three holes punched in the side. I was driving home and got a call that Fox had decided that they want to order four more episodes for this season. They liked the show so much.

And that's really great news because you get paid for the work. But at the same time, okay, so that's four weeks of prep and four more to shoot. And then there's two more of post-production at least. I saw my vacation going away.

So that's really a helicopter problem, isn't it? But at the same time, it's hard work. And then you have to come up with those stories. Okay, what more do we want to say about these people? What can they do? What haven't they done yet? So, you do get to *Night Court*, which is a show I worked on.

A beloved show with our beloved Harry Anderson.

Tom Straw: My beloved Harry Anderson, who I worked with on *Dave's World* also, wonderful to me, we had a great relationship. In fact, I was very close—I won't name a name—but to all but one person on that cast. We were so close, we were a family. And the thing is, it was such fun to go to work there. You'd come up with stuff for Markie to do, John could do anything, you write anything and it's gonna be better when John Larroquette performs it.

Harry the same way. Marsha Warfield, also terrific. I had a little on set joke with her. She replaced Selma Diamond and Florence Halep. So, her first show, when we brought her aboard, we're waiting on Friday night. And we're standing at the snacks table, and I look over at her and I say, "You're feeling all right, I hope?" She laughed. I said, "Because, you know, Eve Arden is in the wings if you're not feeling well."

That's an excellent pull, right? Because that would have been who came next.

Tom Straw: Yeah. But that was one of those magical shows. Getting back to the storytelling, it was like a game for me driving to work. Like I would see a bumper sticker and I would say, "Okay, now how can we make an episode out of that?" We could, and we did, and the writing staff gelled. We had a great leader in the late Reinhold Weege, and we had a cast that could do anything. They could do no wrong. They would take anything and make it better.

I heard recently a bit of room advice from Phil Rosenthal (*Everyone Loves Raymond*). At the end of the season, he would keep everybody for an extra two weeks or something and they'd break like six stories. And then he'd send them off to each write the script he'd assigned them over the summer. And he said, "When we got back in the fall, we were six ahead of everybody. We had to do cleanup, but we already had six finished scripts."

Tom Straw: You want to talk about creating, let's talk about Phil Rosenthal a second. There's in the construct of that show, inspired of course by Ray Romano, but creating a situation that came much out of his own life, meaning Phil's. Honesty. He told honest stories. And when you don't have to do tricks, when you bring your storytelling and—going back full circle here—when you go back to character. Character brings conflict and that's what you want. You don't want to be conflict free, otherwise you don't have a story. But when you have characters whose needs collide, when their baggage gets unpacked on a weekly basis, and you have those performers and that writing and the creation of a Phil. It's gold. What a great show.

It's a perfect storm. So, let's back up. How did Ken Levine give you a break? How did he help you get into TV? And was that a goal or was radio going to be fine?

Tom Straw: I wanted to be Johnny Carson, so I got into radio thinking that would be the way to do it. And I enjoyed it. I liked being in radio. I was okay at it, frankly.

But Ken and I ended up working together at a radio station in San Diego. He had just been fired from a station in Detroit and I had just fired a disc jockey. I was running the station at nineteen or twenty, whatever I was. And I had just dismissed our nighttime disc jockey. I did that over a weekend.

Ken called me on a Monday and said, "I just got fired." And I said, "Do you want to work in San Diego?" And he was there in a couple of days. Let's see Detroit, San Diego. Hmm?

Tough choice.

Tom Straw: So, we had been friends anyway, but that really cemented us together.

And then about a year later, the owner changed formats from Top 40 to Modern Bible (ironically, a week before Christmas). Fired us all. And Ken said to me, I'll never forget the words. He said, "Okay, I don't care if I have to go sell neckties at the May Company, I'm going to break into TV as a writer." And he had a writing partner, David Isaacs, at the time. And next thing I know, they're on *MASH*.

Now, they had a few steps in between, *The Tony Randall Show* and various other things. When I kind of got the itch later to say, "I want to do that too," he read my spec scripts. He gave me comments. I was living in Seattle then, at a radio station. And I actually would fly down to see him over a weekend. And he would go over my script with me and give me some pointers. Very generous, nice guy.

So, then it came time for me to try to get a job. And he was on (I smile when I say this), *AfterMASH*. If you remember that show.

Yes, I do.

Tom Straw: You're one of the few who does.

Ken set it up for me to go in and pitch Burt Metcalf, who was the executive producer. David and Ken would also be in the room. And I went in, and I decided I am not going to leave this office without selling an episode as a freelancer. So, I went with thirty ideas for *AfterMASH*.

Here's the funny part of the story. I was pitching, it was after lunch. And Burt Metcalf was sitting behind the desk in the big easy chair. And I look up from my notes at a certain point and he's fallen asleep. Never a good sign. However, he was listening. It was after lunch, he was a little tired. So, I basically ended up selling my first script to *AfterMASH*.

So let me make sure I understand this: You're in Seattle. You're writing spec stuff. Ken helps you get in the door. You're going to come down to LA. And pitch—you didn't pitch all thirty ideas?

Tom Straw: Yes, I did. And of course, they didn't all fly. Some of them were pretty, pretty not bad. But the one they liked, they said, "Okay, let's do that."

I have a similar story, still one of the weirdest days I ever had. I have a writing partner. We live here in Minneapolis, and we got to know Carl Sautter. Carl was a TV writer. He'd written a book on TV writing. He came through town. We'd won an award for a script, so we got to meet the screenwriter guy.

I handed him a spec I'd written for *Moonlighting*, because he'd worked on *Moonlighting*. He said, "I will take this. I'm not going to give it to *Moonlighting* because they don't care. But I like this, and I'm going to give it to a show I'm working on, which is called *Lucky Luke*." It was a foreign financed hour-long comedy, twelve episodes, starring Terence Hill. You might remember him as Trinity in *They Call Me Trinity*.

Tom Straw: I do remember Terence Hill.

Terence was going to produce and direct and star in twelve episodes in Santa Fe. And they liked the *Moonlighting* script and said, "Come pitch." So, we came up with six ideas—you beat us by five times on that—got on a plane in the morning, flew to LA. Rented a car, drove to Malibu, I think (stopping at an In-N-Out burger on the way), and met them in their rented home.

They were very nice. It was Terence and his wife, Lori. Pitched them the six ideas. Drove back—stopped so my co-writer could put his foot in the Pacific, because he'd never been in the Pacific—got back on a plane and came home. We got a call the next day that said, "Yes, of those ideas, we want to buy one. But also, you know that *Moonlighting* script? Can you rewrite that for an 1800s Western? And of course we said, "Absolutely." And that's what we did.

That whole pitching—going into a room with a bunch of ideas in your head—to have done thirty of them in one sitting, you might be a record setter there.

Tom Straw: It's a harrowing experience. When I eventually later became a showrunner and executive producer of numerous shows, I would always have my heart out to anybody who came in and pitched. I recognized the nerves. I would always try to be receptive as best I could be.

But what happened, just to finish the Ken Levine aspect of this. From *AfterMASH* I got an agent. And the agent got me a free-lance job for a show called *Benson*, writing a spec script for them. I went in and pitched, and they liked one, and so there we are. I turned that in.

And I got a call a couple of weeks later from my then agent saying, "I just heard from Witt-Thomas-Harris productions. They would like to offer you a staff job on *Benson*. They liked your script that much." And I thought, "Well, that's great. Oh my God."

So, the first thing I did is I called Ken Levine and I said, "Hey Ken, congratulate me. I just got offered a staff job on *Benson*." And he said, "Don't take it." And I said, "Why not?" He said, "Because David and I just sold a show, with Mary Tyler Moore starring in it, to MTM. And we'd like you to be on our staff."

And here's where the fun is in the story.

He said, "Here's the problem, though." (I think this might have been March.) He said, "Because of various technical reasons, we are not going to be able to commit to the job for you on paper and pay you until like June. Is there any way you can stall the Witt-Thomas people until we can get some more definition to this? Hopefully sometime this week."

And I thought, "Oh my God, this is a great position to be in, but I'm nervous now." I called my agent back and I explained that to him. And I said, "Is there any way we can stall this?"

He said, "Well, let me see what I can do."

So that was about eleven in the morning. One o'clock in the afternoon, my agent calls me. And he says, "Do you know"—and he mentioned a name. I don't remember the name of this person. His nickname was the Iron Major. He was the business affairs contract guy at Witt-Thomas-Harris. He says, "Well, he dropped dead at lunch today. I think I have your stall."

That's a good agent. That's a really good agent.

Tom Straw: I said, "You know, you're making me a little nervous."

So anyway, lo and behold, I ended up then going with Ken Levine and David Isaacs to work on *The Mary Show*. And that was my first staff job. Then came *Night Court* and various others.

You're on *AfterMASH*, you've written some specs, are you sort of learning on the job when it comes to how to structure and write a script?

Tom Straw: Absolutely. And, you know, frankly, all these years later, I still am. Because it's always a different animal. It's the same animal, but different behavior.

Yes, I've learned lessons. The problem is I forget them sometimes. Or something new comes up. Or I have a revelation. I keep these books right by my desk at all times. I have two little paperbacks here. One is called *The Screenwriter's Workbook* by Syd Field.

Had it for years and years.

Tom Straw: This is my new one, because the other one I could make soup with it, it was so ragged from use. And this one, *The Art of Fiction* by John Gardner, the late great. Both of them late great.

In those two books—and a little bit of *On Writing* by Stephen King—you will find the toolbox.

I read the Syd Field screenplay book as I was thinking of screenplays, but also the tenets are there for structuring television half hours and hours. And I have to tell you, I use the same —I won't say template because I don't do formula—but I use the same guide, the same pillars, if you will, of storytelling in my books.

And it works. It works because it works. And in and around that comes the creative parts. You know, then you weave in the colors and the textures and the characters and the surprises. But those midpoint reversals, the very quick open, the ascending to the climax, and then the very quick resolution. Those things really do work.

And you had the advantage of writing something that actors —within a few days—would say. And you could see it and learn right there on the job going, "Oh, that's how you get from A to B" or, "Oh, that didn't work. Let me try it this way."

Ken Levine has talked about one of his favorite jobs ever was just coming in on a rewrite night. And he said that was just the best. It was a great job. He was doing, I think he said, he was on four shows in one year. So, four nights a week he was out doing that. Looking at what they had, seeing what they did on the stage and going, "All right, here's what's working. Here's what's not. Here's how we fix it." And that just has to get into your writing muscle memory over time.

Tom Straw: It does. When you talk about an education, it isn't just on the page. I'll be glib here and say it's also on the stage. When you go to a run-through and you see what works and what doesn't work, and then you have to go back and figure out why not.

And also, there's a certain amount of tension involved there. I mean, it's not just, "Hey, you know, we'll get to it." No. Tomorrow morning, these people are going to come in and they need a fix. It needs to be right.

And you have to serve all those characters.

Tom Straw: Yes. Not only serve all the characters, not only serve the story, not only have the jokes land, but even things like knowing how to have an actor enter a scene and be able to physically get across a room to do something. You need to give them—Ken came up with this—we called it chuffalog. Sometimes you just have to give them chuffa to say while they go over and do something. Obviously, it's not disposable. But you do need to aid the actor performing the action. They don't rocket across the room. They walk across. So, you have to write so the director can stage all that.

And those are the granular things that you don't really think of when you're holding your index cards of thirty ideas.

I remember hearing Jim Burrows talking about the Norm entrances on *Cheers*. How they had a joke when he came in the first time, and he had blocked Norm to be on the far side of the bar. And then he realized he'd put handcuffs on the writers, who now had to have a Norm joke to make that cross every time.

Tom Straw: Right. But that became a tenet or a big item in the show. I mean, you counted on the "Norm!" joke. You wanted to hear, "How's everything going?" "It's a dog-eat-dog world and my shorts are made of kibble," or milk bone or whatever he said.

The big problem becomes the best part of it, once you solve it.

Tom Straw: Well, that's another thing that Ken and I have talked a great deal about is that problems are good. A lot of writers say, "Oh, geez, I don't want to have to deal with that." And my attitude is, "Let me at it."

Because if I'm bumping into an obstacle, it tells me, okay, something is inherently wrong in the construction of this story or scene. So, I need to either get rid of it, but what I'd really rather do is say, "Well, why is this person, this actor, this character bumping into this?" And you say, "Well, don't go around it, go through it." Confront the situation. And out of those problems often comes your very best writing.

Yeah, but it's scary.

Tom Straw: Yeah, it's scary because you don't have the answer.

I can't prove this. I've had email conversations with Lawrence Block, and I'm convinced that he is making up his Bernie books as he writes them. He's putting himself in the worst corner he can. Because I can't imagine any other way of making them that convoluted unless he was just making it up, which is a scary thing to do when you're 50,000 words in and you don't know how to get out.

Tom Straw: I said to Larry one time, "You know, you really piss me off because I can't really detect any sense of effort." It's like butter, as they say. I've read his short stories. I've read his long form. I've read all sorts of things from him, and he just goes.

He makes it look too easy.

Tom Straw: Yeah. It's effortless. It appears effortless, but I think it was Nathaniel Hawthorne who said, "Easy reading is damn hard writing." He does work at it.

Okay. So, at some point in this TV writing process, you sit down and write your first novel, *The Trigger Episode*. Where did that come from? And how'd you find the time if you're writing for TV?

Tom Straw: Well, of course, there's a story there too. I had been on a show called *Grace Under Fire*.

The aptly named.

Tom Straw: Yes, quite. Let's just call it tempestuous. So, I was off that show, and I came back here to the East coast to write. I just wanted to write screenplays and novels.

And then I get a call from the old production company, Carsey-Werner. So, Tom Werner calls me up and he says, "Would you ever run *Cosby*? Since you're on the East coast." And I said, "No.

You know, as a viewer, I love Bill." (This is before all this stuff came out.) I said, "You know what I've been through? I'm not really ready to do it again." So, he says, "Well, will you at least talk to me?" I said, "Of course."

So, I got back to LA on a trip very shortly thereafter and he held a gun to my wallet. And so, I ended up doing *Cosby* for a while. I signed on for two years and we went until the things ended.

But when that finished, I said, "Okay, now I have time and money. I'm not going to do TV. I'm going to sit out here in my little cottage in the backyard and write the novel I've always wanted to write."

And I thought, what can I write about? And I thought I'm going to turn that experience that I had—and many others combined in Hollywood—and open the vein and let it bleed.

So, I had this idea for a main character who had been a Vietnam combat photographer, loosely based on David Hume Kennerly (who also, by the way, helped me with the book, with research, nice guy), who falls from grace. He took a picture he wasn't supposed to take, got banished from the press corps in Washington, and now he's a paparazzo.

He is now charged by the studio head to go find the missing actress, who tends to go off on benders, so they can shoot the 100th episode, aka the trigger episode which triggers all the profits. So that starts the mystery.

That's where that came from. And I was able to exorcise a lot of the demons. I was able to say a lot of the stuff I was thinking but didn't say when I was running that show and others. And so basically, I found a way to put the star to death in a way that kicked off a murder mystery.

At that point, how do you think you're using your TV writing skills to help you do that first novel? Because it's different. It's the same and different.

Tom Straw: You're absolutely right. You know, one of the things that was astonishing to me, writing my first novel, is I always thought, "Well, this is great. I don't have to worry about fitting it in between commercials and doing twenty-eight pages. I can just go."

In my first draft—even though I tried to structure it (I did go to my Syd Field, and I did go to my John Gardner, and I did go to my Stephen King toolbox, although he hadn't written that one yet)—and I came out with a 600-page manuscript. And I thought, "Well, that's not right." And my agent said the same thing. He said, "You've got a great story in there."

It's amazing how quickly those pages get burned. I spent a summer paring that down, relearning how to get back to square one, which is tight structure. Because I put in a lot of largesse, I guess, in there. There was a lot of prolix. And what I learned very, very quickly—and I have not repeated since—is I learned how many weeks and months I spent writing things I would never use.

And I taught myself—not to hold back—but I taught myself pretty much how to recognize when I was about to go into something that wasn't essential to telling the story. Stop it. Walk away.

Having your background in TV—where if you're going to do an episode, you guys have broken the story, you come up with an outline, you might have had a very detailed outline before you set off to write the script. Did you work that same way? Were you working off a pretty tight outline?

Tom Straw: I was. And I thought the outline was tighter than it ended up being in that particular book. I do believe in outlining, especially in the genre. And this goes to Dickens: you need to work back from where you want to resolve.

Now I frequently outline in great detail, but then I find myself —a third or halfway through the book—kind of veering off that and saying, "Well, now it's going this way." I'll sort of outline on the fly as I go now, instead of going to that document I wrote a month ago.

Some people are pantsers—people who like to do it by the seat of the pants—I don't feel comfortable doing that. I feel really comfortable knowing where the climaxes are, where the act breaks are.

In my new book, *The Accidental Joe*, I very tightly structured that according to the tenets we're talking about and the structure we're talking about. And as a result, it has now sold to Hollywood. Multiple offers, but I chose the one I wanted.

And one of the things that we're delighting in—in the process of developing this now, hopefully finding a home for it on one of the cables or streamers—is that my producing partners have noted, "You know, these chapters, they fall like act breaks and episode cliffhangers. So, if you're doing eight to 10 episodes, this is basically the season."

And that's not an accident. When I did my rewrites, that was a very important part: I wrote it tight, but at the same time, when I went back for my rewrite, I tightened it even more. I'm a very big believer structurally in polarity. I'm very big in believing that on a grand scale and a small scale—even in a scene or in the book itself or a chapter—start one place and go to the polar opposite at the conclusion.

That creates energy, that creates propulsion. And it goes to the surface element that a reader isn't expecting. So that even when you're in a structure, in your own head you're saying, "Okay, I want everything to be cause and effect, but what I need to do is have the effect really flip the narrative so that it propels you to, 'oh my God, what are they going to do?'"

I have a friend who's a playwright who's produced all over the country. He's written tons of plays. He's great at writing mystery plays. And I keep saying to him, you should write a novel. You should write a novel. And his response is "It's too many words." How did you deal with, "Okay, I'm not just creating a structure for a scene and writing the dialogue. I now have to flesh it out." Was that an easy process for you?

Tom Straw: Yes. And I'll say that because, when you're writing to form in a screenplay or a teleplay, you're doing a lot by indication. You're doing a lot cinematically. You're relying a lot on the skill of your actors.

A sidebar here: I worked on a show once with Pamela Reed. I don't know if you know Pamela Reed.

Yes, great actress.

Tom Straw: Super actress. And we were at a run through one day and she came up to me. She had the script and she pointed to a line, and she said, "You know, I can act that. I don't need to say it." And I took out my pencil and I cut the line. That's the difference between prose and doing stage work in any form: Because you can indicate things by inference. And skill.

So, the reason I find it easy to do in books though—particularly the longer I do them—is a lot more of me gets in them. I have a little thing I say to myself: "Notice what you're noticing."

And so, when I am in the middle of a scene or if I have something happening, I'll have a thought about it and I'll say, "Wait a minute, why am I just holding that?" I'll put it down. I'll have the character think it or say it, because it's an observation that maybe the reader is having at the same time. Or maybe I'm a step ahead of the reader and they'll say, "Oh yeah!"

I kind of like filling in those blanks. I just don't overdo it. I want to give the audience credit, the reader credit. But at the same time, I like to let it fly.

I think readers get annoyed with a little too much hand-holding.

Tom Straw: I think there's no doubt about it. Don't empty the dump truck. They don't want to read your research, okay? Research is not entertaining.

Help me on the chronology here. Did *The Trigger Episode* come out before the Castle Books?

Tom Straw: Yes. The story there is that my editor at the publishing house that did *The Trigger Episode*, the book came out. It got very nice reviews, but a German company bought the publishing house because they wanted their nonfiction catalog. Therefore, there was going to be no sequel. There was going to be no more fiction support for that book. So, I thought, "Oh, great. I got my first book made and now I'm dead in the water with a standalone."

But that editor, Will Balliet, he landed over at Hyperion Publishing, which was owned by Disney/ABC. And he took me to lunch one day and he said, "There's a new show coming on called *Castle*. And the lead characters in that are a lot like the couple that you put together in *The Trigger Episode*. Is there any way you would entertain the idea of ghostwriting a one-off kind of gimmick book that we can pretend Richard Castle wrote? And just use that style?"

And I said "Yes," because I liked Will. I trusted Will. I met with Andrew Marlow who created the show. We had instant like.

And so, the idea was that I would write the first book as basically straight to paperback, but here was the thing: They wanted to use the book as a countdown over 10 weeks. They wanted a chapter a week for ten chapters to be the countdown to the premiere of the second season of *Castle*. And they wanted to put them online serializing. This is, this goes back to the old ways of doing serials.

This is Dickens again.

Tom Straw: It's Dickens again. So, I thought that's kind of scary, but I'll do it. I turned in the third chapter and Will called and also Gretchen Young, who is now my publisher for *The Accidental Joe*, called. And she said, "We had a meeting this morning, and we're looking at the chapters, and we think that maybe this is a hardback, not a gimmick."

So, they decided to put a push on it, and they made it a hardback. I finished the book, and it was very well met, and it went to Number Six on *The New York Times*. As a hardback, not as a gimmick, not a throwaway. And then I got a contract for two more.

You ended up doing seven, right?

Tom Straw: Yes. The first one went to Number Six, the second one went to Number Four, and the third one debuted at Number One. And then, all seven were *New York Times* bestsellers, but it was like, "Is this really happening to me?" time. I love the books. I love the story. I love the show. Andrew Marlowe created a great show.

And it's such a great concept.

Tom Straw: It is.

I'm sure there are people to this day who think the guy on the show wrote those books, that he was the writer.

Tom Straw: Andrew and I had a meeting of the minds on the books. I wasn't keen on doing a novelization of what they had already done, and neither was he. And so, we talked about it over cocktails one night. And what we came up with was, let's make this book not *Castle*. Let's make it—the premise of the show was that Richard Castle, who is a big time, best-selling writer had lost his muse. And so, he was going to do research by doing a ride along at a police station and he falls in love with his guide, Kate Beckett.

Andrew said, "What if this were the idealized version of Richard Castle's experience in the show?" So, it isn't the show. It's not the stories of the show. It's like, for Richard Castle, what would the product of that research be? And that's really what the books were.

I came up with my own stories. I put little Easter eggs in the books, so that people would see that I'd watched it. It was a thrill to write. I enjoyed every minute of that. It was really fun writing.

And to go back to the first book where I had to write it quickly as a serial. I described it to Andrew Marlowe that every chapter was like throwing a mailbag off a train. Because I would finish a chapter and it would go out. And it forced me—because I was working daytime at *The Late Late Show* then as a writer—so I wrote 9 p. m. to 2 a. m. I would write when I got up at home.

It forced me as a writer not to be so careful. It forced me to trust my instincts because I couldn't wait. I couldn't sit there and smoke a pipe and sit back with brandy and say, "Well, what would they do here?" I had to be productive. I had to crank it, but I didn't want it to be cheap and bad. So, what I did was I just said, "If you have an idea, that's your idea. Go. And see where you can take it. And trust yourself." And it changed all of my approach to writing.

That takes a lot of trust though.

Tom Straw: Yeah, it's scary. It's a high wire act. And funny things happen.

Like for instance, when those ten chapters were posted online, I still had ten more to do to finish the book. And when I got to chapter seventeen, I realized I'd written myself into a corner. So, I had to repurpose some of the clues from the early part, because I decided to have it end a different way.

You talk about the outline. I got there and the story was going a different way. So, I had to kind of say, (I'll make this part up), "Okay, it wasn't a hammer. It was a screwdriver." Or I'll have him use the hammer in a different way.

What I'm saying is, I got to the end, and I had to repurpose things, so that it would all fit. Because I couldn't go back and say that never happened. It wasn't *Dallas* after all.

I think high wire act is the best way of describing that. I remember when Stephen King was putting out *The Green Mile* and he didn't know where it was going to end. So, it sounds like you really enjoyed being a ghostwriter. Is there a downside to that position?

Tom Straw: Of course there is. But of course, now the mask is off, and it's known. There's also a certain amount of protection there, because if it hadn't worked, you know?

But there were funny situations. When the first book came out, my wife and I were in Boston, and we were at a restaurant for lunch on Newbury Street. And this is like one of those Marshall McLuhan moments from *Annie Hall*. We're sitting there having lunch. And at the table behind us, there's a man explaining to his wife, "No, you see, he doesn't actually write the books."

The guy was talking about *Castle*. "It's not really him that writes the books. He's the actor that plays the guy who writes the books, but we don't know who writes the books." And I was so tempted to turn in my chair and say, "Perhaps I can be of some help here."

So, the ghost thing is kind of like nutty too. But I never bristled because frankly, when you're writing TV, you're ghostwriting, aren't you?

Yes. Nobody knows who wrote what on a show generally. So as a TV writer, you have to take notes from the producer or from the network. And novelists have to take notes from their editors. How did you learn to take notes and the best way to take notes from your TV work?

Tom Straw: Well, first of all, most of the notes you get in TV are infuriating. And I have to say that. It's not just writer defensiveness. Rare is the collaborator you get who understands the material. I mean, it's not really even a matter of "Oh, they don't like it." It's a matter of, they don't get it. They don't understand.

And so frequently when you're in notes, you have to sort of restrain yourself, because everyone you get, you need to kind of like take them to school and you can't keep doing that. So, you learn to say, "Well, thank you very much. I'll take that under advisement." And then you just don't.

A term that we used on a show I worked on, we *differentize* it. We take the note, and we just make it look like we did something with it. "Oh, we like what you did there on page eight. Yeah, that's wonderful." Or we just keep it the same and put a star on the page next to it, which indicates to the reader that a change was made.

Sometimes you do get very constructive notes. Sometimes you do get the perspective of somebody who really does have integrity and understanding of craft and storytelling who recognizes that, you know, "If you did this here, it might do that. Or this isn't happening, can you go back?"

The thing about getting notes in books versus TV is that generally you get fewer notes. They tend to be more holistic. And they are asked in the form of a question. "Have you ever considered that maybe dot, dot, dot?"

One of the joys of working on *Castle* was working with Andrew Marlow, who was the creator of *Castle*. You know, he's busy doing his show. So, I would—when I had half a book done—I would send it to him and then I would keep writing. And so about two weeks later, we'd have a note session, and we'd turn pages. And the thing is, I had been a showrunner. I spoke his language. He is a great writer. He speaks mine. (I'm not saying I'm a great writer. I'm saying he is.)

So, our collaboration was seamless. I mean, it was amazing. We would turn pages. I'd have my binder on the table, and he'd be in LA, and I'd be back here. We would turn pages on the manuscript, and he would seriously do things like, we'd be on page fourteen, and he'd say, "Okay, let's skip ahead to page eighty-two." He knew that he could say just a little and I would know what to do with it.

The only hard note he gave me was on the second book when he said, "I figured out on page thirty who the killer is." And he was right. And he said, "That's not good." And I said, "You're right." So, I found a way to hide that better. Nothing's perfect, but that's why you collaborate.

But the thing is I had a creative partner—both in Gretchen Young at the publishing house and Andrew Marlowe on *Castle* —that was like, we all kind of saw the same thing. We all respected each other's ups and downs, and it was a joyful experience. And not a lot of rewriting, I might add. Just simply because we talked it out first.

I think one of the things that I've run into talking to TV writers who have gone on to write novels is they are really surprised in the note process from an editor or a publisher. That these are generally suggestions, you don't have to do them. And like you said, they're in the form of a question and they're designed really to make you think.

I have nine books in my series. In the first four, I had a publisher for them, and then I bought them back. But in editing those first four books, I can only think of one note she gave me where she said, "I really think you need to change this." Everything else was, like you say, in the form of a question, getting you to think about, is there a better way to do this? Is this too confusing?

I think it's great that you had the experience of getting impossible notes in TV, which prepares you for anything when it comes to getting notes from an editor.

Tom Straw: My first session of getting notes on that first *Castle* book—I won't name any names—I was in my office at *The Late Late Show* and Andrew Marlow was on the conference call with me and studio executives. It began this way: One of the notes from the studio executive was, "I don't understand why they're at this restaurant outside where the murder took place."

And I said, "What do you mean?" "Well, it's outside." And I said, "Yes, but the man fell from a high building down onto a sidewalk cafe."

And the note was, "Shouldn't you say that?" So, I'm sitting there, holding my temper, saying, "If you look on page two, it says, 'Nicky Heat approaches a sidewalk cafe.'" You know what their response was? "Maybe you should say it twice."

So, from that point on, I had my butt cheeks clenched into an asterisk for the rest of that call. And I received an assurance after the call—very quickly from Andrew and others—that they would never put me through that again, that I would get my comments directly from him.

You mentioned just in passing there that you're working full time for Craig Ferguson while you're writing this. I imagine there are many novelists who are—as I was—working a full-time job when they're working on a novel. How did you juggle that? That's got to be a very long day.

Tom Straw: It was crazy. In fact, two weeks ago yesterday, I did Craig's podcast. And I was talking to him about that, because he kind of knew I was doing it, but he really didn't.

So here was my day: Ten a. m. I'm at the conference table at CBS with Craig and the other writers. And we're talking about what kind of sketch are we going to do in the show tonight? And what's the topic going to be for the monologue? What's going on in the world that we can talk about? Things like that.

And then we'd write sketches, and we'd pitch in on the monologue that he would come up with and shoot the show, be done at six p. m. There's no post-production because it's a live talk show/comedy show.

I would then leave the studio. I would grab dinner very quickly. Head home to my rental apartment in Burbank. Call my wife, who is here on the East Coast. I'd talk with her until—you know, the time difference—she's ready to go to bed.

Nine o'clock p.m., I'm in the chair at my desk in the apartment, starting to write the *Castle* book. Write from nine p.m. until two or three in the morning, until I could go no further. Sleep for three, maybe four hours.

And at seven a. m., I'm on the internet, seeing what's going on, so I would have ammunition for that day at Ferguson.

Yes, because you can't just walk in at ten a. m. without having a satchel full of stuff.

Tom Straw: Yes, you've got to be ready. You're pitching.

It's funny, when I told that to Craig on this podcast, he goes, "You were doing all that?" And I said, "Yeah, why do you think my work habits were so bad?"

It was rigorous, and what I told myself at the time: first of all, I was loving the writing. I was loving the work. But I told myself, I can't live my life like this, but I can live a mission like this. And I saw myself on a mission. And so, I did that. The first three books I wrote, I was still on the Ferguson show writing them.

That is a very full day.

Tom Straw: Yeah. Exhausted. And a lot of like catch up naps on the weekend and all that, just to kind of muscle through.

But then again, as I told you earlier, it forced me to rely on my instincts as a writer and to say to myself, "I don't care that I'm tired and it's 12:30 a.m. I need to do another two hours. I've got to get to this point to stay on my schedule."

That's discipline.

Tom Straw: Yeah. And that's the thing I think I would say about —to take the biggest picture look at your examination here, which is TV and books—the discipline of writing for television. The need to meet a deadline. Because those actors are going to be sitting there the next day and they want a script and you're paid to do that.

And so, the discipline of knowing that deadlines are not variable and that you need to perform. And you need to not only meet the deadline, but you need to meet the deadline with your very best work. And that then went into books, I hope.

It appears to have worked.

Tom Straw: So far.

Finally, for any aspiring novelist whose reading this or listening to this, do you have one final piece of advice you'd give them based on your experience writing TV that'll help them as a novel writer?

Tom Straw: If you're trying to break in, my advice to you would be treat it like a job. Don't just aspire. Don't say, "Hey, I'm going to write a book someday," or "I'm going to write it." You need to be productive, because when you are productive, that's where the momentum comes from.

I think that would be the best advice I could give to any writer would be: write.

AFTERWORD

Alright, let's wrap this up.

Thanks for sticking with me through all these interviews with novelists who also write for TV and movies. A big thanks as well to all the writers who made time to chat. Doing these interviews was a delight.

While every reader will likely take away their own treasures from diving into these insightful conversations, here are twelve things that stuck out to me as potentially useful for fellow novelists:

1. Actively observe the world around you and mine those details for vivid descriptions.

2. Study and understand story structure fundamentals like inciting incidents, rising action, climaxes, etc.

3. Write with narrative momentum—end chapters/sections in ways that propel readers forward.

4. Develop each character's distinct voice through effective dialogue and narration.

5. Find a writing process that works for you, whether outlining extensively or discovering organically.

6. Schedule consistent writing time and hold yourself accountable to deadlines.

7. View editorial notes as opportunities rather than critiques—stay open-minded.

8. Balance straightforward prose with artful embellishments and descriptions.

9. Draw from your own experiences and perspectives to ingrain authenticity.

10. Read works across genres to expand your versatility as a writer.

11. Embrace collaboration by joining a writers group or finding beta readers.

12. Persist through rejection and writer's block—doggedness is key.

As I think back on the illuminating conversations captured in these pages, I'm more convinced than ever of the value in novelists looking beyond the realm of prose fiction for story-telling insights and inspiration. Exploring the hard-earned wisdom of these filmmakers has been a revelation, reinforcing just how many of the guiding principles behind unforgettable movies and TV shows can be adapted to create equally compelling novels.

From the conceptual heavy-lifting done in pre-production, to the crucial creative choices made during filming and editing, to the savvy strategizing required to distribute and market the finished product—at every stage, the parallels to the novel writing process are striking.

While a screenplay and a book manuscript may look very different on the page, the fundamental building blocks of story remain the same: A keen understanding of narrative structure, a well-developed cast of characters, an attention-grabbing opening, an emotionally satisfying ending—these are the common denominators of storytelling success, regardless of the medium. By borrowing from the best of big-screen storytelling, we can bring a cinematic sensibility to our novel writing.

I'm endlessly grateful to the generous and talented writers who shared their stories and insights in these pages. I hope their perspectives have inspired you as much as they have me, and that they've opened your eyes to new ways of looking at the craft of fiction writing.

So, dream big, write boldly, and when in doubt, ask yourself, "Hey, what would a screenwriter do in this situation?"

John Gaspard

www.albertsbridgebooks.com

THE POPCORN PRINCIPLES UNLEASHED:
A WORKBOOK FOR NOVELISTS

Capture Cinematic Magic - Infuse Your Novel with Hollywood's Best Storytelling Techniques

This hands-on workbook offers a treasure trove of exercises directly inspired by cinematic techniques to captivate your readers from the first page to the last. Learn how to create characters that resonate deeply, master pacing that keeps readers on the edge, and weave visual descriptions that turn prose into an immersive movie of the mind. From crafting the perfect opening to delivering satisfying plot twists and callbacks, this workbook is your guide to creating stories that stick. Perfect your narrative with guidance on cutting excess and deepening themes, ensuring every word counts.

Elevate your writing with the expert tips and tricks contained within 'The Popcorn Principles Unleashed.

Grab it today!

https://www.albertsbridgebooks.com

THE POPCORN PRINCIPLES

Take your novel to the next level.

Unlock the power of the silver screen with The Popcorn Principles, a guide to fiction and novel writing.

It will help you Craft unforgettable characters ... Write compelling scenes ... Hide exposition ...Structure powerful endings

With this book (and the movies it draws on), you'll learn the tools and techniques used by screenwriters, which you can apply to your own writing.

Craft your next novel and become a better writer with The Popcorn Principles. (Popcorn not included.)

Grab it today!

https://www.albertsbridgebooks.com

GET YOUR FREE ELI MARKS SHORT STORY BUNDLE

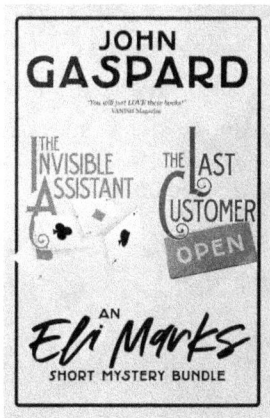

The Eli Marks Short Mystery Bundle
"The Invisible Assistant" & "The Last Customer"
Two short-story cozy mysteries in one!

"You will just LOVE these books."– VANISH Magazine

The Invisible Assistant

There's no question it was murder. But who killed whom?

What begins as a typical corporate event for magician Eli Marks turns into a twisted mystery when he is called to the site of a recent murder/suicide. Confronted by the details of the grisly crime scene, Eli must sort through the post-mortem clues - and the bickering of the officials as well as a poorly-timed allergy attack - to determine just who murdered whom.

The Last Customer

The request was a first for Eli Marks: "Can you help me make my tuba disappear?"

Magician (and magic shop owner) Eli Marks is confronted with this odd demand just before he is about to close up shop for the day. Over the next few tense minutes, he finds a solution to that question which also, fortunately, puts him the positive side of what turns out to be a life-or-death situation.

Click HERE to grab your free copy!

Or go to www.elimarksmysteries.com

JOIN THE NEWSLETTER

Keep in touch about all the books at Albert's Bridge books — The Como Lake Players mysteries ... the Eli Marks mysteries ... plus occasional deals on other mysteries! And no spam!

Click HERE to join!

ABOUT THE AUTHOR

John is author of the Eli Marks mystery series as well as several other stand-alone novels, including *"The Sword & Mr. Stone," "A Christmas Carl," "The Greyhound of the Baskervilles"* and *"The Ripperologists."*

He also writes the *Como Lake Players* mystery series.

In real life, John's not a magician, but he has directed six low-budget features that cost very little and made even less—that's no small trick.

He's also written books on the subject of low-budget filmmaking. Ironically, they've made more than the films. Those books *("Fast, Cheap and Under Control"* and *"Fast, Cheap and Written That Way")* are available in eBook, Paperback and audiobook formats.

John lives in Minnesota and shares his home with his lovely wife, several dogs, a few cats and a handful of pet allergies.

Find out more at: https://www.albertsbridgebooks.com and https://www.elimarksmysteries.com.

facebook.com/JohnGaspardAuthorPage

x.com/johngaspard

instagram.com/johngaspard

bookbub.com/authors/john-gaspard

BOOKS BY JOHN GASPARD

Stand-Alone Novels
THE SWORD & MR. STONE
A CHRISTMAS CARL
THE GREYHOUND OF THE BASKERVILLES
THE GREYHOUND & GATSBY
A GREYHOUND INVESTIGATES THE MYSTERIOUS
AFFAIR AT STYLES
THE RIPPEROLOGISTS

Filmmaking/Writing Books
THE POPCORN PRINCIPLES
MORE POPCORN PRINCIPLES: THE SEQUEL!
THE POPCORN PRINCIPLES UNLEASHED: A WORKBOOK
FOR NOVELISTS
THE POPCORN PRINCIPLES STRIKE BACK
FAST, CHEAP AND UNDER CONTROL
FAST, CHEAP AND WRITTEN THAT WAY
TELL THEM IT'S A DREAM SEQUENCE
WOMEN MAKE MOVIES